Compiled by Angela R. Edwards

PEWS & PERSPECTIVES

Worship Experiences That Shaped Our Faith

Foreword by Pastor Abie Kulynych
of City of Refuge Fellowship Church

PEWS & PERSPECTIVES:

Worship Experiences That Shaped Our Faith

Compiled By:

Angela R. Edwards

Foreword By:

Pastor Abie Kulynych

With Contributions By

(in order of appearance):

Marlowe R. Scott
Terrace V. White
Angela R. Edwards
Simone "Iman" Holyfield
Min. Tosha R. Dearbone
Reyna Harris-Goynes

Pearly Gates Publishing, LLC, Harlem, GA (USA)

Pews & Perspectives:
Worship Experiences That Shaped Our Faith

ISBN 13: 978-1-948853-91-0 (paperback)
ISBN 13: 978-1-948853-92-7 (eBook)
Library of Congress Control Number: 2026939207
Printed in the U.S.A.

For information and bulk ordering, contact:
Pearly Gates Publishing, LLC
Angela Edwards, CEO
P.O. Box 639
Harlem, GA 30814
PearlyGatesPublishing@gmail.com

Dedication

To you, the reader, whose footsteps have echoed in both familiar and new pews:
Your story matters.

Every moment you've spent in worship, whether filled with joy, struggle, or transformation, is a vibrant thread of hope woven into faith and community.

Your pew worship experiences are not just memories; they are testimonies worth sharing, honoring, and passing on.

As you turn these pages, may you feel inspired to reflect deeply on your own journey—on the moments that shaped your faith, the wounds that needed healing, and the victories that renewed your hope. Remember that your story has the power to motivate others, foster connection, and create a sense of belonging within the family of believers.

Acknowledgments

First and foremost, giving all honor and glory to God. Just when I was about to throw up my hands in defeat, He whispered, "I am not done with you, My child." *Pews & Perspectives* is truly a product of HIS doing... HIS making. The men and women who are a part of this project were chosen—by HIM. When others fell away, they remained for the assignment, and I am GRATEFUL.

I am deeply thankful to **Pastor Abie Kulynych** of City of Refuge Fellowship Church in Burlington, New Jersey, for his quick and enthusiastic "YES!" to contribute the foreword. His heartfelt insights and pastoral wisdom greatly enhance this anthology, strengthening its message of faith, healing, and community. His support for both me and this project has been invaluable in shaping *Pews & Perspectives'* influence. Blessings today and always, Pastor Abie. You are loved and appreciated.

To **Marlowe R. Scott**: Mom, I value your steadfast faith, decades of service to the church, and parenting. Your testimony of enduring through trials and leadership challenges offers profound wisdom and encouragement, reminding us all that faithful perseverance is a powerful witness to God's sustaining grace and limitless love. I love you!

To **Terrace V. White**: Thank you for sharing your powerful story of divine calling and transformation. Your vivid encounter with God and your ongoing dedication to walking the sometimes-narrow path offer a compelling voice of courage and renewal, inspiring readers to respond boldly to God's persistent call. Blessings, my friend.

To **Tosha R. Dearbone**: I honor your courageous testimony, Sissy, of faithful service amidst church hurt and healing. Your journey of obedience and discernment offers vital insight into the complexities of the church community and the power of God's restoration, while also providing hope to those experiencing similar struggles. Thank you for sowing seeds of hope into others. I love you!

To **Reyna Harris-Goynes**: Thank you, Sis. Reyna, for your raw and inspiring account of God's divine protection and transformation. Your story of surviving a traumatic experience and choosing wisdom adds to this collection with a powerful reminder of God's providence and the importance of trusting His guidance in every situation. Sending lots of love to you and yours!

To **Simone "Iman" Holyfield**: Sis. Simone, thank you for sharing your honest journey from ritual to an authentic relationship with God. Your story of searching, stumbling, and ultimately embracing real faith adds depth and encouragement, showing that a true connection with God is always within reach, regardless of how long the journey takes. I appreciate and love you!

Finally, to **every reader** whose heart this book touches: May each day be filled with joyful reflection for the gift of life. Contemplate the stories, scriptures, and prayers within, and embrace them as your own. Then, when God gives you the "GO," I pray you will be ready to march confidently into His calling for your life—without shame.

Foreword

I grew up in church. My grandfather was a pastor, my father always took part in some form of lay ministry, and my mother was a missionary. We faithfully attended services on Sunday mornings, some Sunday evenings, and most Wednesday nights. I went to a Christian school. I remember many nights watching preachers on TV, and it was not unusual for missionaries to visit our home. I don't recall a time when church wasn't central in my life, but that doesn't mean I've always been *happy* about it.

Like everything else, if we've been part of a church for any length of time, we probably hold both good and bad memories. We've likely learned a lot—both what to do and what not to do—from those we've worshipped with. We've probably laughed and cried, been encouraged and mistreated, and seen the good, the bad, and the ugly. While we often try to tell our stories *carefully*, I believe it's paramount that we tell them ***truthfully***. God's grace is best revealed in the whole story, not in sanitized versions.

There's a reason the Scriptures tell us about Abraham's faith and his fear, about David's tender and hard heart, and about Peter's confession of faith and how he had to be rebuked by Jesus. Nothing is ever just one thing, and although part of a story will guide us, it won't show us the full way. After his repentance, David wrote in Psalm 51 that God desires truth in our inward parts. Jesus said that the truth would set us free, so let's tell the truth! Let's share our stories because our stories are the church's stories. The victories and failures, the wounds and the healings, the love and the not-so-loving... they all come together to form a tapestry that proves, time and again, God truly does make everything beautiful in its time.

The first pew instance I remember was a wooden one in a small country church where my grandfather was the pastor. I have vivid memories of sitting beside my grandmother as we sang hymns, then listening to my PaPa preach. The next experience I recall was one in which I got caught playing underneath the pew during Sunday evening service, even though I was supposed to be sitting still and paying attention. (I also remember the foyer where I was spanked and told to go sit back in that pew.) A few years later, I sat in that same pew during a baptismal service. We had brought a friend from my class who had never been to church before. He sat on the edge of his seat and, as the pastor baptized the first person, my friend jumped to his feet and yelled, ***"He dunked him!"*** My Dad was much more patient with my friend than he had been when I was caught playing under the pew.

To be honest, my memories are more about the rooms I was in than the pew experiences. I clearly remember standing next to my father as we sang songs like "How Great Thou Art," "Great is Thy Faithfulness," and "Our God Reigns." I can close my eyes even now and hear him singing, *"Majesty, worship His majesty, Jesus who died, now glorified, King of all kings,"* and I'm right back in that room. I also think about the outdoor camp meetings in the summer, and I start sweating just thinking about them.

I think of the first time I can remember—I mean, really remember—sensing what everyone else called "God's presence." It was at our home church in Richmond, Virginia. A choir from an area Christian drug rehabilitation center came, and as those men sang, I knew they had met God. I knew that God was there with us because He was truly alive in them.

My perspective might differ slightly from others. I've had the privilege of worshipping in hundreds of churches representing many denominations, cultures, and countries. As a pastor, I've led my congregation in worship for decades, but I've also enjoyed preaching at other churches in our community and in different states. As a supporter of missionary work, I've had the opportunity to worship in churches in Kenya and various parts of the Philippines. I've attended services where the language was foreign, and some where the liturgy felt strange. I've experienced churches that seemed quite "normal," and others that had no formality at all. I've stepped into churches on the other side of the world and instantly felt at home. Conversely, I've been in some close to home that felt like I might as well have been on the other side of the world.

My worship experiences also include singing along with congregations led by whistles, drums, full bands, guitars, pipe organs, and no musicians at all. I've been at church services where the congregants walked for hours to get there, some came on horseback, and others who journeyed for several days. No matter where I've been, I've never been to a church where there wasn't someone who was glad when they said, "Let us go to the House of the Lord."

I've been in auditoriums for concerts that turned into churches for a few hours. It was during one of those concerts-turned-worship services, when the band finished playing and the lead singer started preaching, that Jesus captured my heart, and I gave Him my life. I was 16, grew up in the church, and had prayed the 'Sinner's Prayer' more times than I could count, but when that particular man preached that night, the Holy Spirit did something through him and something in me that changed everything. I didn't just meet Jesus that night; I saw Him in all His beauty and majesty. Suddenly, I knew He was the Son of God and the King of kings. I didn't just ask Him to forgive me of my sins; I surrendered my heart to Him. He had given all of Himself for me, and I gave all of myself to Him.

Throughout my life, I've seen God do incredible things in His many different "houses." I've witnessed miracles that can't be explained away, like the time I was in Kenya when a blind man was helped into the church and walked out with his sight restored. We were in our home church in Virginia when God started to heal my father of cancer. I was in a service in Tulsa, Oklahoma, when God said, "You've given Me your heart, now give Me your life," and called me into ministry. It was again in Kenya, during the heat of the day, when I watched sores disappear from the bodies of little children as my wife prayed for them. I was in the Philippines when a man testified that he had been a violent man but was now a follower of Jesus. I've watched God heal marriages, renew minds, restore friendships, and break bondage.

Time and again, God meets people as they gather in His name.

Since this is a time for 100% transparency and honesty, I must mention that I've also seen some things in the church that weren't so great.

We've all heard gossip, complaints, and foolishness inside the church. The truth is, we've probably been victims of them or willing participants. We've likely seen some things that, in hindsight, were just funny, heard some songs that shouldn't have been sung, or perhaps listened to singers who shouldn't have grabbed the mic. Have you been to a service where a "joyful noise" was taken too literally? "Bless their heart," we'd say. Sometimes, we act peculiar—but not like a royal priesthood or a holy nation. God is still working on us, though, even as some of us might be working against Him.

If you've been in church for a long time, you might carry both the imprint of love and the scars of hurt.

We've also observed and heard many things that were seriously wrong, such as hearing God's Word used in ways that do not reflect His heart or character at all. We've seen bully pulpits, false theology, and the Lord's name taken in vain. As an aside, using the Lord's name in vain doesn't mainly mean saying "God" or "Jesus Christ" casually or irreverently, but rather attaching God's name to things He has no part in. If you've ever attended a church business meeting, you've probably seen God's people lose their composure and, at times, their sanctification when the "business" of the church is discussed.

Throughout my years sitting in the pews, I believe the most meaningful moments in church happen after the service is over. It's when the final "Amen" is spoken, and we step into our communities that the church truly comes alive. Acts 2 shows us that the first church dedicated itself to the apostles' teaching, fellowship, and prayer. In essence, they were dedicated, committed, and faithful to God's Word, His people, and His presence. The church isn't just a place we visit or what occurs when we gather there; it is the people of God living from His Word, for His glory, and in His love.

I've experienced God most often when sitting at tables with brothers and sisters in Christ, in hospital rooms during the joy of birth and the pain of death, at birthday and graduation parties, during urgent phone calls when prayer is needed, in the laughter of fulfilled promises, and through the tears of deep disappointment. Church isn't just three hymns and a sermon: it's sharing our hearts, our lives, and our love with each other.

In Romans 12:4-5, the Apostle Paul wrote that the church is one body made up of many members. Then he added, *"We belong to each other."* If we are in Christ, we are God's children, and we are brothers and sisters to one another. No, we don't have the same DNA, but we've all been washed by the **same blood**, we have seats waiting for us at the **same table**, and we have rooms in the **same House.** We don't always "get it right," but when it's right, there's nothing like it. Jesus said in John 13 that if we love one another, the whole world will know that we are His disciples.

I've seen men rally around a widow and her daughter after the death of their husband and father, spending themselves for them because they loved their brother in Christ. I watched firsthand, after my wife had a miscarriage, as her sisters in Christ came to our home, lay in her bed, wept with her, prayed for her, cleaned our house, took care of our son, and brought us meals as we mourned. I've seen people open their homes to brothers and sisters with nowhere to go, give from both abundance and scarcity to pay funeral expenses for a family member of a brother or sister in Christ, care for each other's children, visit and pray with each other's elderly parents, and celebrate victories both great and small. I've seen the church genuinely be the church, and when it does, there's nothing like it.

And I've seen the church fall short. I've been lied about and betrayed, misunderstood and overlooked. But just as much, I've spoken harshly and been impatient, jealous, and immature. *We're being honest here, correct?*

Far too often, the church has been a safer place for abusers than victims. It's been skilled at cover-up to protect itself rather than trusting God to guard His church while we faithfully care for the wounded. We've loved money. We've thirsted for power. We've fallen short of the glory of God, the example of Christ, and the standard of love. We've all sinned, yet Jesus promised that the gates of hell will not prevail against

His church. He promised to return for her [the church] and make her spotless and pure. He also promised that He would be with us always, even to the end of the age.

So, my brothers and sisters in Christ, how should we respond to all these diverse, sometimes seemingly conflicting perspectives? I pray that we'll give them the respect they deserve. I pray that as you read the different perspectives in this book, you'll add them to yours, and that we will all see together that the church is beautiful and flawed; filled with truth and often swayed by lies; separate and set apart yet still influenced by the culture of the world we live in; beautiful and scarred. The church still is and will be these things until Jesus returns—where the lost come home, the broken find healing, the blind receive their sight, and the dead in sin find new life in Jesus. The church is also where the saved are still being sanctified, where those who know better are still learning to do better, where love covers a multitude of sins, and where church people still need to be more like Jesus.

I pray that we honestly examine the pews we grew up in—the ones God used to shape us—and that we decide to be part of creating another generation of faithful saints of God. I pray that we do better than those who came before us and that we pray for those who come after us to do greater things. Most of all, I pray that we choose ***Pews and Perspectives*** that fit us and allow God to use His church to further shape His view of us and those around us.

Be blessed today, tomorrow, and forevermore!

Pastor Abie Kulynych

Abie Kulynych, Lead Pastor
City of Refuge Fellowship, Burlington, New Jersey
www.cityofrefugefellowship.org

"Do not be deceived, God is not mocked; for whatever a man sows, that he will also reap. For he who sows to his flesh will of the flesh reap corruption, but he who sows to the Spirit will of the Spirit reap everlasting life. And let us not grow weary while doing good, for in due season we shall reap if we do not lose heart."

Galatians 6:7-9 (NKJV)

Preface

There is something sacred about a pew. Not just the wood itself, although some are beautifully crafted, cushioned for comfort, and worn smooth by generations of faithful congregants. The sacredness lies not in the furniture, but in what happens there. Prayers are whispered in desperation. Tears of both joy and sorrow are shed. Then, there are those moments when Heaven seems to break through and touch the earth. Pews witness our transformations, questions, doubts, and homecomings.

Pews & Perspectives: Worship Experiences That Shaped Our Faith is a collection of those moments. Inside, there are raw, honest, and deeply personal testimonies from people who have sat in pews across decades and denominations, through seasons of spiritual awakenings and times of profound hurt. They are not sanitized stories made to make church life seem perfect. They are real accounts from real people who have wrestled with God, leadership, the community, and ultimately with themselves as they sought to understand what it means to follow Jesus in an imperfect world full of imperfect people.

The title of this book prompts us to consider two aspects of the Christian journey: the pews where we physically gather and the perspectives we develop as we encounter God and each other in those sacred spaces. The pews act as classrooms where some of life's most vital lessons are learned—not always from the pulpit, but often in quiet moments of observation, through painful experiences of betrayal, exhilarating encounters with the Holy Spirit, and the slow, steady work of staying faithful when everything around us seems to be falling apart. Our perspectives are shaped by what we observe and experience, as well as how we choose to respond when our faith is tested.

On these pages, you will meet a woman who crawled beneath the pews as a curious child, only to have a life-changing encounter with the Holy Spirit as a teenager that shaped her entire spiritual journey. You will walk alongside someone who has faithfully served for over 80 years, witnessing the evolution of church life from wooden benches to padded seats, from strict traditions to Spirit-filled revivals, and from moments of deep community to painful times of leadership failure. You will stand with a man who heard God's call on a Sunday morning—a voice so clear and commanding that he could no longer stay frozen on the pew. There are other stories within that are sure to speak to your faith journey in one way or another, and it is our collective prayer that you receive what is meant just for you.

These stories span generations, denominations, and locations. They include experiences in African Methodist Episcopal churches, nondenominational congregations, megachurches, small family-run ministries, and online worship communities. Yet despite their differences, they share common themes that will resonate with anyone who has ever called a church "home" or struggled to find one.

Every story in this collection testifies to the transformative power of encountering God. Whether it happens in a back pew during a revival service or in the sacred waters of baptism, transformation is the heartbeat of genuine faith. These storytellers remind us that conversion is not always a single moment but often a series of moments, and that transformation can be both immediate and lifelong.

The church is meant to be a place of belonging, and these stories celebrate the beauty of genuine Christian community. You'll read about a grandmother who made sure her grandchildren attended Vacation Bible School every summer, a mother who sang in the choir and served as an usher while raising children in the faith, a friend who invited another to church and grew together spiritually, and so much more. It's the power of "the village" that helped raise and discipline children, while faith circles provided fellowship and support.

The community is also where some of our deepest wounds happen. These stories don't shy away from what many call "church hurt"—the pain that occurs when the very people who should guide us fail to do so. Even then, it remains possible to love the church while recognizing its brokenness.

Perhaps the most powerful theme woven throughout these testimonies is perseverance: the conscious choice to keep believing, seeking, and serving, even when it might be easier to walk away. A prime example is the minister who submitted her resignation with tears in her eyes, choosing obedience over comfort while trusting that God would heal the wounded parts of her that only He could heal. Perseverance is not about blind loyalty to institutions or leaders; it's about a deep, abiding conviction that God is faithful even when people are not.

These stories also remind us that faith is intergenerational. We see it in the grandmother who ensured her grandchildren attended church, in the mother who made sure her children were rooted in the Word and knew and loved God, and in the adult children and grandchildren who now worship alongside their parents. The contributors to this book understand they are links in a chain. They are recipients of faith passed down from previous generations and are now stewards responsible for passing it forward to the next. This legacy perspective influences how they face both trial and triumph. The question is not "What kind of faith will I have?" but "What kind of faith will I model and leave behind?"

As you read these stories, you'll likely see yourself in them. You may remember childhood moments of swinging your feet in pews, or a specific time when God called your name and you had to decide whether to answer. You might also carry wounds from church hurt or be in a season of searching for a spiritual home where you truly belong. No matter your age—20s or 80s—your faith journey could just be beginning, and we understand that without judgment. Wherever you are on your spiritual journey, these stories provide companionship. They say, "You are not alone in your questions, doubts, disappointments, or joys." In fact, they invite you to reflect on your own pews and perspectives—those places where you have encountered God and the viewpoints shaped by those experiences. You are encouraged to be honest about the complexities of church life, grieve what needs grieving, celebrate what deserves celebration, and continue moving forward with hope.

The pews you have sat in—whether wooden or cushioned, in grand cathedrals or small storefronts, in physical buildings or virtual spaces—are part of your story. The perspectives you've gained through sermons, songs, transformations, and trials have shaped how you continue to grow. This book honors both pews and perspectives, trusting that God uses all of it to draw us closer to Him and each other.

May these stories inspire you to keep seeking, believing, and trusting that the God who plants seeds in childhood will bring them to full harvest in His perfect time. May they give you permission to acknowledge your pain while still holding onto hope. And may they remind you that every pew holds the potential for an encounter with the Living God... if only you have the eyes to see and an open heart to receive.

Welcome to *Pews & Perspectives*. Welcome home.

"Then they cried out to the LORD in their trouble, and He delivered them out of their distresses. And He led them forth by the right way, that they might go to a city for habitation. Oh, that men would give thanks to the LORD for His goodness, and for His wonderful works to the children of men! For He satisfies the longing soul, and fills the hungry soul with goodness."

Psalm 107:6-9 (NKJV)

Introduction

If walls could talk, church walls would have the most compelling stories to tell. But since they can't, we must rely on the voices of those who have sat within them: the faithful souls who have occupied pews across decades, denominations, and life stages—each carrying their own questions, hopes, wounds, and revelations. *Pews & Perspectives: Worship Experiences That Shaped Our Faith* is a chorus of those voices. This is a collection of testimonies that reveal what happens when ordinary people encounter an extraordinary God within imperfect communities.

This book is not a theological treatise or a step-by-step guide for church growth. It is something much more meaningful: a collection of genuine human experiences that reveal the beautiful, painful, messy, and transformative aspects of living out the Christian faith within a community. These are stories from the front lines of church life.

The title of this book reflects its dual focus. "Pews" represent the spaces where we gather for worship. They are the furniture of our faith—the designated places where we show up week after week, year after year, sometimes out of genuine hunger for God and sometimes out of sheer habit or obligation. They are more than just furniture; they symbolize our commitment to gathering, belonging, and participating in something larger than ourselves.

"Perspectives," on the other hand, represent the mental and spiritual lenses through which we interpret our experiences. Our perspectives are shaped by everything we encounter in those pews: the sermons that pierce our hearts, the songs that uplift our spirits, and the moments when Heaven seems to break through the ordinary, touching us in extraordinary ways. Our perspectives evolve as we mature in faith and learn to distinguish between God's voice and human voices. It is then that we discover that following Jesus often requires us to make difficult choices that cost us something.

The stories in this book span more than eight decades of Christian experience, from the 1940s to today. They cover geographic boundaries from small towns in New Jersey and Louisiana to the large cities of Houston and Atlanta. They cross denominational boundaries, including African Methodist Episcopal traditions, nondenominational churches, megachurches with thousands of attendees, and close-knit family ministries. They include both in-person worship and online church experiences that became vital during the COVID-19 pandemic.

Yet despite that diversity, these stories share striking commonalities. Each person wrestles with fundamental questions: How do I know God is real? What does it mean to surrender my life to Jesus? How do I stay faithful when church leaders let me down? Where do I belong when the community I trusted betrays me? How do I pass on faith to the next generation? And perhaps most importantly: How do I keep believing when everything around me suggests I should walk away? They are not abstract theological questions debated in seminary classrooms. They are questions wrestled with in real time by people whose faith was forged in the fires of lived experience.

One of the most striking revelations in these stories is how faith formation truly works. We often see it as a straight-line process: we hear the gospel, believe, get baptized, and then live happily ever after with unwavering faith. The testimonies shared here show a much more complex and realistic picture.

Faith starts with seeds planted long before we realize they are growing. A child crawls beneath pews during church service, soaking in the atmosphere even though she can't understand the words. A young girl swings her feet and eats peppermints to stay quiet, unaware that something is taking root in her spirit. A young man feels the pull of God's Spirit for months before finally responding to an urging during a Sunday service that changes everything.

Each story teaches us that God is both patient and persistent at the same time. He plants seeds in childhood that may not sprout until adolescence or adulthood. He surrounds us with His Spirit long before we become aware of His presence. He calls our name again and again—gently at first and then with more authority until we finally answer. The process of forming faith is not a single moment; it's ongoing. It involves observation, questioning, resistance, surrender, growth, testing, and continual recommitment.

Perhaps the most challenging topic mentioned is the paradoxical nature of the Christian community. On one hand, we see the church at its best, reminding us why it matters. We aren't meant to follow Jesus in isolation. We need the songs that uplift our spirits, the teachings that challenge our thinking, and the prayers that sustain us. We need to see faith modeled by those who have walked the path before us, and we must model it for those who come after us. The church, at its best, is a beautiful expression of the body of Christ: diverse members working together, each using their unique gifts for the common good.

Conversely, these stories reveal the church at its worst. We encounter a strict organist who values rules more than grace, leaders who overlook real concerns, drama and false rumors that spread easily, and mean-girl spirits that infiltrate leadership. The communities that vow unconditional love sometimes love us only under certain conditions, based on our behavior, appearance, or willingness to stay silent about issues. That is the paradox: the same institution that can bring us closest to God can also cause our deepest wounds.

The contributors in this book do not provide easy answers to the paradox. They don't say, "Just find the perfect church," because they recognize that such a thing does not exist. They don't claim, "Church doesn't matter; just have a personal relationship with Jesus," because they understand the biblical call for community and the practical benefits of gathering with other believers. Instead, they demonstrate something more valuable: the ability to hold tension and love the church while acknowledging its brokenness.

If these stories ended with pain and disappointment, that would be tragic, but they do not. These testimonies remind us that our stories are still unfolding. God is still writing, working, healing, and leading. The wounds we bear are not forever; they are opportunities for God's healing power to shine through. Each story, in its own way, bears witness to God's faithfulness to restore, heal, and lead us "home."

As you read the following stories, you are invited to do more than just observe from a distance; you are invited to remember your own pews—the ones where you first encountered God, experienced transformation, got hurt, or found healing. You are encouraged to reflect on your perspectives and how they have been shaped by your experiences, changed over time, and influenced the way you see God, the church, others, and yourself. You might find yourself inspired to answer a call from the Lord that you've been resisting, to leave a situation that is damaging your soul, or to keep going when you feel like giving up.

Whatever your reason or response, know that these stories are offered as gifts. Not as prescriptions for how you should live out your faith, but as testimonies of how God has been faithful in the lives of ordinary people navigating the extraordinary journey of following Jesus. May they encourage, challenge, comfort, and ultimately point you toward the One who sits not in the pews but on the throne... the One who calls each of us by name and invites us to "come on home."

"Behold, I stand at the door and knock. If anyone hears My voice and opens the door, I will come in to him and dine with him, and he with Me."

Revelation 3:20 (NKJV)

Table of Contents

Experiences That Shaped My Faith

Marlowe R. Scott

Bio: Marlowe R. Scott is married to Andrew Scott and is a mother, grandmother, and great-grandmother. A retired government employee, she enjoys writing stories and poetry, crocheting, doll collecting, and quilting. Recognized for her writing since high school, Marlowe is an international bestselling author and has co-authored numerous works. She has also written blogs for the Battle-Scar Free Movement, a nonprofit supporting victims and survivors of domestic abuse. Her church service includes roles as choir president, Sunday school teacher, Atlantic City District President for the A.M.E. Lay Organization, and Pastor's Steward at Friendship A.M.E. Church in Browns Mills, NJ.

Dedication: Appreciation to my daughter, Angela Edwards, who publishes my stories, the Methodist Sunday school, and the teen group teachers. Most recently, Rev. Abie Kulynych, Pastor of City of Refuge Fellowship, and his wife, Melissa, have added to my spiritual growth. Love and thanks to my Christian family and friends who encourage me.

"What has been will be again, what has been done will be done again; there is nothing new under the sun."
(Ecclesiastes 1:19)

"PEWS"

The title of this book immediately grabbed my attention! It made me think more deeply than I expected, raising the question: What role do pews play in shaping faith? After a few days, my mind started coming up with answers.

Before sharing my experiences and stories, I must point out that the word "pew" is not found in the Holy Bible, although some modern revised Bibles may include it in their interpretations. The word developed after the 11th-century Norman Conquest. At that time, pews were raised seats designed to provide seating during lengthy sermons. By the 17th century, "pew" referred to any bench with a back used by multiple worshippers.

As I reflect on my life, I notice the many years and the different types of seating in the churches I've attended. Most often, pews were used in pulpits, for choirs, and for church officers such as deacons, as well as for special events. Most were wooden with backs and cushions. Some churches used folding metal chairs or wooden chairs, with or without padding. Pulpit areas usually featured large, carved padded seats. In the church, seating has improved over the years. During Jesus' early ministry, people sat on stones, logs, and the ground. As centuries passed, seating evolved into what we have today.

I have personal stories about church pews and chairs that changed how I participated because of seating arrangements. The most upsetting was at an A.M.E. church. I was very active and sang with the senior choir. The strict organist didn't allow anyone to sing during the Sunday service unless they had attended choir rehearsals.

One Sunday, I was in church helping the Sunday school teachers. I heard the choir rehearsing upstairs. After assisting one of the older teachers in putting things away, she asked if I was going to join in singing with the choir. I told her no and explained that the organist didn't allow anyone who missed choir rehearsal to sing during the Sunday service. The older woman assured me it would be fine and told me to get my choir robe and follow her upstairs. WHAT A MISTAKE! When I passed the organist to enter the choir box, she called me back, "reminding" me that I hadn't attended choir rehearsal and couldn't sing that day. I told her the older member said it would be okay to go up with her. WRONG! I was told (in no uncertain terms) that I could not participate. I turned around, tears in my eyes, sat on a seat in the hallway, and cried.

The result? Church officers later called and asked what happened. After explaining, they invited me back, but I decided to leave that church with my three children and never return.

I also remember another problem with pews at a different church I attended. The need arose to get new pews, more than what was previously in the sanctuary. To encourage members to donate, it was suggested that engraved family names be attached to the side of the pews along the aisle. Soon, issues surfaced. Donors who had their names on the plaques believed they owned the pews and didn't want others to sit on them. To prevent further arguments and disagreements, the engraved names were removed.

I must pause here a moment before continuing my story. Many members of my current church want two services every Sunday, but the pastor and some of the officers want only one. Different suggestions are being made about many changes to service length. In addition, the names of organizations have been changed, and some have been removed entirely. At the time of this writing, nothing has been finalized or approved one way or another.

Getting back to my pew stories...

There was an older woman who liked the same seat every Sunday. One winter, she had a coat she wanted to leave on the back of the seat next to her. When the church filled up, an usher asked her to please move the coat, roll it up, and put it on the floor or hang it in the church's coatroom. She refused to do any of those things, took her coat in her arms, walked down the center aisle toward the doors leading to the steps, and left the church.

Another personal experience was when I decided to leave the A.M.E. church in my town. I had been a member for years, sang in the choir, taught Sunday school, ushered, served as President of the Atlantic City District Lay Organization, and was the Pastor's Steward. One Sunday, I saw a woman and a man take funds from the offering after church as I headed to the back office to count the money. I told the pastor about what I witnessed, identified who they were, and was told she would "take care of it."

I waited several weeks, but the pastor never responded to my concern. The issue kept me tossing and turning every night. One night, while in bed, I heard a clear voice telling me to leave the church and relinquish my duties as the Pastor's Steward—which I did. Eventually, I was blessed to find another church to worship at.

There are ongoing discussions and debates that people have been having for years: whether worship services should be held on Saturdays or Sundays. It has been said that Saturday is the Sabbath Day—the day of rest—on our calendars, with Sunday being the first day of the week. That argument never bothered me because I believe that we, as Christians, should participate in various activities daily, including but not limited to:

- Praying.
- Attending Bible study.
- Reading and studying scriptures.
- Giving—as time and talents allow.
- Supporting church ministries.
- Participating in events.

Many pastors have contributed to my spiritual growth over these past 80+ years, but one stands out in particular. A few years ago, a guest pastor, Rev. Abie Kulynych, from the City of Refuge Fellowship (CORF) church, taught our Wednesday night Bible study. His voice commanded attention, and his teachings were clear. Right away, he caught my interest. Since then, I have watched his Saturday evening services online and met his family and church members, who are friendly and respectful. They have supported the sales of my Christian literature and accepted my donations toward their CORF ministries and building renovations. Rev. Kulynych's wife, Melissa, is a lovely Christian and supporter. Their two sons, Noah and Elijah, are also active in the church alongside their parents.

In a recent online post by CORF, the following words were shared (please read and digest the last four lines in particular):

"God forbid

that I chase after things

He turns me away from.

God forbid

that I hold onto things

that He's trying to rid from me.

God forbid

that we live our lives

chasing things that He died

to free us from."

There's an old song we used to sing in churches I attended that says, "Every day is a day of thanksgiving. God has been good to me. Oh, yes, He gives us victory. So many people doubt Him. I can't live without Him. That is why I love Him so. He's so real to me."

As you can see, my "pews" experiences are things that touch, excite, and bless me, even those that caused me pain in some way. I pray you find that you are not alone on this spiritual journey.

"PERSPECTIVES"

A simple definition of "perspective" is: A specific way of viewing something shaped by your experiences and beliefs—a mental lens, if you will, that influences your understanding or the ability to see things in true relationship with each other.

Life's desires, needs, understandings, and sufferings are different for everyone. I encourage you to attend a church where the Holy Spirit leads and inspires you—and be committed. There's a song I was taught in my youth that states, "Dare to be a Daniel, dare to stand alone, dare to have a purpose firm, dare to make it known." An appropriate "perspectives" quote by Rev. Billy Graham reads, "We are the only Bible the world is reading.

We are the creeds the world is needing. We are the sermons the world is heeding."

A personal family situation had a big impact on my life, and it involves the passing of a loved one. Yes, death can be a sad time, but some funeral services are filled with loving words, happy memories, and good times about the person who passed away.

The first person close to me who died and whom I loved dearly was my father. He was a farmer in his late 40s, blessed with many talents. He built our brick house on over 12 acres of land while I was still in grade school. He also dug wells, farmed some of our land, repaired my stick-shift Chevy, and much more.

In the late 1950s, he began sawing tree limbs into logs for heating our home and the immigrants who lived in the area during the winter months. One late Sunday afternoon, after church and dinner, he went into the woods to cut down more trees. He was accompanied by a couple of migrants at the time. After a while, a tree fell the wrong way and knocked him out. The men went to tell my mother, and the ambulance came to take him to Bridgeton, NJ Hospital. My two brothers rode in the car with my mother as she followed behind.

I was not home when the accident happened. When I arrived, my neighbor was the one who told me that my father was in the hospital. I got into my car and drove as fast as I could safely. The emergency nurses directed me to where my family was. My father was in a room, not yet awake but still breathing on his own. After a brief visit, our family sat outside his room for five or six hours. The doctors didn't give us much hope that my father would survive.

My father died in the early hours of the next morning. For the first time, I heard what is known as "death rattles" in his throat before he passed away. After grieving our loss, we eventually left the hospital and headed home, crying along the way.

At this point, I will move on to the funeral preparations and service...

My father was an active member and officer at John Wesley Methodist Church in Bridgeton, NJ. My mother was also very involved; she was a Sunday school teacher, sang with the senior choir, and more. Since the new pastor didn't know my father well, my mother asked if the former pastor—who knew my father—could deliver the eulogy. The homegoing service was well conducted and spiritual. His favorite song, "Life is Like a Mountain Railroad," was sung at the service:

"Life is like a mountain railroad,

With an engineer that's brave.

We must make the run successful

From the cradle to the grave.

Watch the curves and hills and tunnels;

Never falter, never fail.

Keep your hand upon the throttle

And your eyes upon the rails.

Blessed Savior, thou wilt guide us

'Til we reach the blissful shore,

Where the angels wait to join us

In thy praise forevermore."

The family, church members, and other attendees were full of "Amens." When it was time for the final viewing, THE UNEXPECTED HAPPENED! The current pastor stood up and started rambling. The deacons, officers, family, and visitors had nervous looks on their faces, along with restless movements in their seats. The undertakers, who were preparing to open the casket for the final viewing, stopped walking up the aisle. It was a very uncomfortable moment for all of us. After a few minutes of the pastor attempting to describe my father and his church activities, the casket was finally opened. The ministers, officers, family, and other attendees gathered around, hugged each other, and wept.

Later, during the repass, some members and friends shared their frustrations with our pastor's words, while others did the same throughout the following week. One surprising reaction came from an ordained minister whose feelings were unexpectedly conveyed.

"Submit yourselves to God. Resist the devil, and he will flee from you" (James 4:17).

The following scripture from James 2:2-5 tells of people dressed in fine clothes and a poor man wearing filthy, old clothes.

"Suppose a man comes into your meeting wearing a gold ring and fine clothes, and a poor man in filthy, old clothes also comes in. If you show attention to the man wearing fine clothes and say, 'Here's a good seat for you,' but say to the poor man, 'You stand here,' or 'Sit on the floor by my feet,' have you not discriminated among yourselves and become judges with evil thoughts? Listen, my dear brothers and sisters: Have not God chosen those who are poor in the eyes of the world to be rich in faith and to inherit the kingdom He promised those who love Him?"

The Sheepfold – A Poem

Marlowe R. Scott © 2015

Being a part of THE LORD'S SHEEPFOLD
Is a very blessed thing.
Because of Redeemer, Jesus,
Is the Keeper, Savior, and King!
When we are lost, Jesus finds us.
He picks us up and carries us back.
With Him as Protector and Leader,
No good thing shall we lack.
He is tender, gentle, and kind.
He loves us and calls us each by name;
Surely, Jesus knows the pastures we need
To maintain our native and earthly frames.
We can sleep peacefully at night
Under the Shepherd's watchful eye.
The dawning of each new day
Guarantees that He is still nearby.
Do not be caught outside THE SHEEPFOLD;
There are dangers and deaths out there!
Come and stay safely inside with us
Until we transcend to eternity in the air!

****

The following Church Covenant was adopted and previously used during communion services:

“Having been led, as we believe, by the Spirit of God, to receive the Lord Jesus Christ as our Savior, and on the profession of our faith, having been baptized in the name of the Father, and of the Son, and of the Holy Ghost, we do now, in the presence of God, angels, and this assembly, most solemnly and joyfully enter into covenant with one another, as one body in Christ.

“We engage, therefore, by the aid of the Holy Spirit, to walk together in Christian love to strive for the advancement of this church in knowledge and doctrine.

“In the case of differences of opinion in the church, we still strive to avoid a contentious spirit, and if we cannot unanimously agree, we will cheerfully recognize the right of the majority to govern. We also engage to maintain family and secret devotion; study diligently the Word of God.

“To guard each other’s reputation, not needlessly exposing the infirmities of others; to participate in each other's joys, and with tender sympathy, bear one another’s burdens and sorrows.

“To cultivate Christian courtesy; to be slow to give or take offense, but always ready for reconciliation, being mindful of the rules of the Savior in the 18th chapter of Matthew, to secure it without delay; and through life, amid evil report, and good report, to seek to live for the glory of God, who has called us out of darkness into His marvelous light.”

For many years, the covenant was read aloud and accepted. Sadly, the new pastor’s reactions to the recitation sparked many questions and misunderstandings, so he decided to end that tradition during communion services.

Jesus, My Friend Jesus – A Poem

Marlowe R. Scott © 1995

What a Friend we have in Jesus;
He all our sins and griefs will bear.
Our Friend Jesus came and left someone special
When He ascended to His Father in the air!
The Comforter—the Holy Spirit—
Surrounds each of us every day and everywhere,
Because our Beloved Counselor and Friend, Jesus,
Left the Holy Spirit here when He joined His Father in the air!
But wait! Do you really know my Friend Jesus?
Does He all your burdens bear?
Are you really ready to meet and greet Him
When He descends again, coming down through the air?
If not, then I invite you today to receive Him
And enjoy the friendly, bountiful LOVE I share
With our Lord and Savior—Jesus Christ—
Who reigns in Heaven with God, up there in the air!
Come quickly! Praise and celebrate with me!
A Friend who loves unconditionally, without compare;
His name is Emmanuel—Wonderful Jesus.
Be ye ready to meet Him
When He comes again from glory,
Shouting through the air!

****

As I finish the poem, I pray you will be inspired to seek a deeper connection with Jesus also... until it's time to rise to your Heavenly home. May my words and stories, written in "Experiences That Shaped My Faith," spark reflection and a better understanding of those at home, work, church, or in other activities.

A Prayer of Faithful Endurance and Divine Guidance

Gracious and Eternal God,

We come before You with hearts shaped by decades of experiences, some filled with joy and others marked by disappointment, yet all woven together by Your faithful presence. Just as seating has evolved from stones and logs to cushioned pews, You have carried us through every season and offered rest for our weary souls, no matter the physical space we occupy.

Father, we thank You for the gift of longevity and the privilege of witnessing Your faithfulness across generations. We are grateful for the Sunday school teachers who planted seeds of faith in young hearts, for choir directors who taught us to lift our voices in praise, and for pastors whose clear teachings captured our attention and brought us closer to Your Word. Thank You for those spiritual teachers who not only preached truth but also lived it authentically.

Yet, Lord, we also bring before You the painful memories—those moments when we were publicly humiliated and turned away from serving You, when tears flowed in church halls because human rules overshadowed Your grace. We remember the times we witnessed wrongdoing and spoke truth, only to be met with silence and inaction. We recall the nights of tossing and turning, wrestling with whether to stay or leave, until Your voice broke through the darkness with clear direction. Thank You for being our Shepherd even when earthly shepherds failed us and for giving us the courage to walk away from what was harmful. We are grateful for the blessing of wisdom to find new pastures where our spirits could be fed.

We praise You for being the God who sees and notices when offerings are mishandled and when traditions are dismissed without understanding their significance to Your people. You are the righteous Judge who calls us to treat all people equally, whether they wear fine clothes or filthy rags or sit in the front pew or stand in the back. Forgive us for when we have shown favoritism, valued position over people, or allowed our preferences to create barriers in Your house.

Lord, we pray for those who are navigating church transitions and disagreements—those caught between differing visions for worship services, organizational changes, and shifting traditions. Grant wisdom to pastors and officers as they lead Your sheep. Give congregations patience and grace as they adapt. Help us remember that while methods may change, Your truth remains constant, and our unity in Christ transcends our differences.

We also thank You for the gift of family. Thank You for fathers who built homes with their own hands and taught us the value of hard work, for mothers who served faithfully in multiple ministries, and for children and grandchildren who carry forward the faith we've modeled. Comfort those who have heard the death rattle of a loved one, sat through uncomfortable funeral services, and carry the weight of grief even years later. Remind them that You are near to the brokenhearted and that our loved ones who knew You are safely in Your presence.

In Jesus' name, we pray. Amen.

"So, I will restore to you the years that the swarming locust has eaten, the crawling locust, the consuming locust, and the chewing locust, My great army which I sent among you. You shall eat in plenty and be satisfied, and praise the name of the LORD your God, who has dealt wondrously with you; and My people shall never be put to shame."

Joel 2:25-26 (NKJV)

"Trust in the LORD with all your heart, and lean not on your own understanding; in all your ways acknowledge Him, and He shall direct your paths."

Proverbs 3:5-6 (NKJV)

An Encounter with God

Terrace V. White

Bio: Terrace V. White is a Richmond, Virginia-based author of the International Bestselling books *Parenting Memoir: From the Heart of a Single Father* and *Poetic Spirit: Resurrecting the Voice Within*. He retired from the United States Air Force in 2000, received the Gene Ackers Father of the Year Award in 2008 for Henrico County, Virginia, and retired from the Federal Government after 20 years of service in 2021. With a charismatic personality, he is a dedicated father committed to integrity and excellence. Terrace loves connecting with others and inspiring them to set and reach their goals. Connect with him at teedub46@yahoo.com and follow him on Instagram @terracewhite7.

Dedication: To the loving memories of my grandparents, Arthur and Mary Parson, and to all my aunts and uncles for laying a solid foundation and being Godly examples. Also, to my grandchildren, Blaze and Phoenix: May the God of hope fill you with peace as you learn to trust Him.

"Then Peter said to them, 'Repent, and let every one of you be baptized in the name of Jesus Christ for the remission of sins; and you shall receive the gift of the Holy Spirit.'"
(Acts 2:38, NKJV)

Christianity often plays a central role in family life across many parts of the world, especially in the southern United States. Its deep-rooted presence helps shape a sense of community, togetherness, awareness, and expression, and contributes to forming a long-lasting personal belief system that most people carry with them throughout their lives. No matter where you travel or settle in your adult years, those fundamental Christian influences and traditions can always be linked to personal resilience and success.

Like many others who grew up with similar core beliefs, my story is not much different from yours. The long church services, special gatherings, songs, prayers, foods, snazzy hats and outfits, and, more importantly, studying and believing in the Word of God all help bind our diverse families and cultures.

In today's society, people often go through their day rushing from task to task and stressing over the circumstances around them. Their thoughts tend to run on autopilot, and they rarely take time to reflect on their lives or ask questions like, "Why am I here?" or "Does God have a specific plan or purpose for my life?" Surely, there must be more to life than what we see in the natural world, yet day after day, we allow life to dictate how we act and react.

Some people grow tired along the way before they finally decide to "seek, ask, and knock" for help. They may begin by asking a family member or close friend for advice, but soon realize that even good advice doesn't fill the emptiness inside. Often, just when they think they are about to break completely, a breakthrough occurs instead. The breakthrough might be small, but it's usually marked by the quiet, gentle voice of God.

I still remember the exact moment on a Sunday morning in February 1994 when that quiet, small voice of God called my name. For months, I felt the strong, powerful pull of God's Spirit surrounding me. There was no doubt in my mind that it was His Spirit. Who else would command such attention and show such a personal interest in me? Although I hadn't physically seen Him, I could see and feel the works of His power in my life and in the lives of others around me. That intense feeling demanded a sense of urgency, and it wouldn't go away. *(I didn't want it to.)* As time went on, I found myself wanting something more and more. I couldn't quite put my finger on it, but I knew something was missing.

That particular Sunday morning began like any other, with a quick breakfast and then heading to church. Little did I know this Sunday would be a different, memorable day that would change my life forever and for the better.

It was at the end of the service during the altar call when the 'magic' happened. All heads were bowed, and in a loud, angelic voice, the preacher said, *"Is there anyone here today who knows that God has been calling them to surrender their life to Him? He is calling you to walk away from your past life... no matter what you have done. He's calling you to give your life to Jesus."* Although I had heard the preacher say those exact words numerous times, week after week and month after month, they hit differently that time. I immediately knew both the preacher and the Spirit of God were talking directly to me as if I were the only person in the church or in the whole town, for that matter.

With my head bowed and eyes tightly closed, I heard a voice call out, *"Terrace, come."* At first, I acted as if I hadn't heard anything. Then I heard it again: *"Terrace, come."* By then, I knew who was calling me and why, but I couldn't move. I felt frozen, as if super-glued to the seat. I couldn't move an inch. The voice inside my head grew louder, and with authority, it said, ***"Come! Now!"*** I popped up out of my seat like a Jack-in-the-box. It happened so quickly, as if something had completely taken over my body. Previously, I was able to control all my emotions in response to similar prompts, but that time was different, and I was determined to answer!

As I stood there, shaking by my seat, I was overcome with a feeling of nakedness. I wasn't ashamed or afraid, however, because I wanted to bare and surrender it all. I was one step closer to the voice that called my name—the same still voice that I'd recognized from before but foolishly chose to ignore.

The voice called out again: *"Come! Now!"* That time, my right foot involuntarily moved forward, and my left foot reluctantly followed. As I kept placing one foot in front of the other, that involuntary left-right rhythm became easier, even as the road ahead seemed to stretch longer and longer. What had felt like miles of walking with the dead was, in actuality, only a few steps to the end of the row.

Suddenly, I was thrust out into an opening, as if someone had pushed me from behind into a moving train. I briefly looked back, but there was no one there. The row of people I had just slipped past and stepped on their feet had disappeared. The row seemed to have been walled off, as if it was never there.

I found myself standing in the middle of the church aisle. It was like standing in a foggy, green open field early in the morning. A sense of peace washed over me like I'd never felt before. Envision with me an aisle covered with plush red carpet and lined with flowers in many brilliant colors, each with a sweet, unrecognizable aroma—so tempting I wanted to reach out, grab a handful, and taste them. Their lingering scent lifted me as if I were on a magic carpet. I was no longer afraid because, for the first time in my life, I had fully surrendered.

Stumbling like a toddler, I made my way to the front of the church. I heard that same still, small voice whisper, *"Trust Me."* My awkward left-right cadence responded to the moment, and I stepped forward with confidence and purpose, even as my feet felt like I wore cement shoes. I kept moving forward with my eyes wide open, looking straight ahead, not to my left or right.

About halfway down the aisle, I thought of the story of Peter walking on the water. I remembered his dilemma when Jesus told him to get out of the boat and "come" to Him on the water. As soon as Peter looked down at the churning water below his feet and took his eyes off Jesus, he started to sink. That's when he cried, *"Master, save me."* I realized I needed to keep my eyes fixed straight ahead at Jesus and trust that it was His voice calling my name.

I kept moving forward on weak, shaky legs. The closer I got to the front of the church, the heavier my feet felt. It was like walking in quicksand, and the pit seemed to stretch on like an empty pier. Still, with a clear mind and a determined heart, I was committed to pushing through because there was no turning back!

Those last few steps felt lighter and lighter, and I finally reached the front of the church. In a toddler-like manner, I had sidestepped all those imaginary obstacles that stood in my way. The self-doubt, lies, pride, unbelief, and many others of Satan's tactics and schemes had been exposed and were no longer a threat—at least on **that** Sunday morning.

While still in a bit of a trance, I heard claps and cheers coming from behind me. As they grew louder, all my senses sharpened, and I became even more focused. With my eyes fixed on the preacher, he stretched out his hand as if passing a baton for me to run the final lap of the race. I acknowledged his gesture with a big, goofy grin before reaching out my hand with great pride to give him a firm handshake, then a bear-like hug as the claps and cheers intensified. I didn't want to let go of his hand, much like when Jesus extended a helping hand to Peter. I slowly turned around to see where the ruckus was coming from. To my surprise, the congregants had risen to their feet and were genuinely overjoyed with my decision—a decision to answer the call of my name.

The moments afterward were a complete blur. I remember being swiftly led to a back room to change from my church clothes into a thin, white, one-piece gown-like outfit. The white outfit symbolized purity, renewal, and a renewed commitment to faith. It was very fitting for the occasion. As I slipped into it, I thought about John the Baptist baptizing Jesus in the Jordan River, and I became overwhelmed with emotion because I knew I was in the right place and had made the right decision.

My excitement and anticipation grew stronger as I approached the small pool of water behind the plush burgundy curtain used for baptisms. The water in that sacred pool was lukewarm but not very deep. I anticipated its cleansing power even before I stepped in.

I felt a warm sensation spread through my body as the preacher placed his hands on my shoulder. It was as if I had been filled with a surge of uncontrollable energy—a burst that ignited a flame yet to be consumed. Still in a daze, I bowed my head, crossed my arms over my pounding heart, and pinched my nose with my right hand. The preacher asked, *"Do you believe that Jesus is the Son of God and that He died for your sins?"* I responded with a resounding ***"Yes!"*** that echoed throughout the church. I then surrendered every fabric of my mind, body, and soul to the Holy One sent from above.

Almost simultaneously, the preacher forcefully dunked my nearly limp body backward into the water. What felt like a full minute only lasted two seconds. Just as quickly as I sank into the water, I was lifted up as a new creation with a fresh start. In an instant, my old life had passed away.

The water in my ears temporarily muffled the claps and cheers as they grew even louder than before. As I stood there, no longer confused, I could not help but wonder if the Spirit of God had come down and shone His light on me, like a dove flying from the sky. Either way, I had finally answered the call, and it happened exactly where it was supposed to, as was written before I was naturally born.

Since that early Sunday morning in February 1994, my life has been forever changed, and my name has been written in the *Book of Life*. I keep my eyes fixed straight ahead while trying to walk that narrow path. I admit that I sometimes unwittingly stray from the path, have often fallen short of my earthly calling, and occasionally stubbornly try to face life alone without the One who called and saved me. It is only through God's grace, mercy, and conviction that I am continuously redirected back on track, thereby strengthening my future both here on earth and in eternity.

Over the years, I have lived an exciting and blessed life. Surrendering my life to Jesus was the best decision I've ever made! Being baptized was just the beginning. I must make daily choices to surrender and follow Him, not my own will. The one constant I can always rely on is that God has always been with me, and He will never leave me. I have never doubted His love, promises, presence, or forgiveness because I know and believe in them. Any discipline I've endured may not have been pleasant at the time. Still, I can honestly say it was well-deserved because I drifted out of alignment by "doing my own thing" or "giving in to my own desires," which was a direct result of acting on my own understanding.

Glory be to God, for we serve a God who loves us enough to both save and discipline us. He provides a way and provisions for everything we face. To believe in Jesus means to have a confident conviction that He is who He says He is, will do what He promises, and by trusting in Him, we enter a personal, eternal relationship with the Son of God! Therefore, we are never alone, will find rest in Him, experience true peace, and discover lasting spiritual fulfillment.

My prayer is that you also find Jesus—our greatest source of hope—and experience His grace, mercy, goodness, love, and peace!

"For it is written: 'As I live,' says the Lord, 'every knee shall bow to Me, and every tongue shall confess to God.'"
(Romans 14:11, NKJV)

A Prayer of Surrender and New Beginnings

Heavenly Father,

We come before You with grateful hearts, acknowledging that You are the God who calls us by name. Not as strangers in a crowd, but as beloved children whom You know intimately and pursue relentlessly. Thank You for the quiet, gentle voice that breaks through the noise of our busy lives... that still, small whisper that refuses to be silenced until we finally answer, "Here I am, Lord."

Lord, we praise You for Your patient persistence. Throughout all our days, You surround us with the powerful pull of Your Spirit, creating an urgency within our souls that demands attention. Even when we try to ignore Your call and remain frozen in our seats, paralyzed by fear and hesitation, You do not give up on us. You keep calling: "Come. Come now." Thank You for loving us enough to pursue us until we finally surrender.

We confess that we have heard Your voice many times before but have chosen to ignore it. We have sat through countless altar calls and heard the same messages week after week, yet we hardened our hearts and controlled our emotions. Forgive us for the times we acted as if we hadn't heard You and foolishly chose our own way over Your perfect plan. We acknowledge that there comes a moment when Your voice grows louder, and Your authority breaks through our resistance until we can no longer remain seated in our comfortable places.

Father, we thank You for those life-changing moments when everything shifts, and we finally decide to respond. We praise You for the courage to stand, even when we feel exposed and vulnerable, because we know that surrendering everything to You is the only path to true freedom. Thank You for the supernatural strength that moves our hesitant feet forward, one step at a time, even when the road ahead seems to stretch on forever.

Lord, we remember those who walked this path before us: grandparents, aunts, and uncles who laid solid foundations and set Godly examples. We are grateful for the Christian influences and traditions that shaped our belief systems, including the long church services, special gatherings, songs, and prayers that brought our diverse families together. May we honor their legacy by passing this faith to the next generation. May our grandchildren's grandchildren learn to trust You and be filled with the peace that comes from knowing You.

We pray for those standing in the middle of the aisle right now, caught between their old life and a new beginning, surrounded by fog but feeling Your peace washing over them like never before. Remind them to keep their eyes fixed straight ahead, not looking down at the churning waters of doubt or to the left and right at distractions. Like Peter walking on water, may they trust Your voice above all others and keep moving forward on weak, shaky legs, knowing that each step brings them closer to You.

Lord, guide us in making daily choices to surrender to and follow You, rather than our own will. When we unintentionally stray from the narrow path, fall short of our earthly calling, or stubbornly try to face life alone, redirect us through Your grace, mercy, and conviction. Discipline us when needed, for we trust that Your correction comes from love and keeps us aligned with Your purposes.

We pray for those rushing through their days on autopilot, stressed by circumstances and never pausing to ask, "Why am I here? Does God have a specific plan for my life?" May they experience a breakthrough when they feel like they are about to break. May they hear Your quiet voice calling their name and have the courage to answer.

Thank You for being a God who never leaves us and whose love, promises, presence, and forgiveness are constant. May we find rest in You, experience true peace, and discover lasting spiritual fulfillment as we walk this faith journey.

In Jesus' name, we pray. Amen.

"And Peter answered Him and said, 'Lord, if it is You, command me to come to You on the water.' So, He said, 'Come.' And when Peter had come down out of the boat, he walked on the water to go to Jesus. But when he saw that the wind was boisterous, he was afraid; and beginning to sink he cried out, saying, 'Lord, save me!' And immediately Jesus stretched out His hand and caught him, and said to him, 'O you of little faith, why did you doubt?'"

Matthew 14:28-31 (NKJV)

"Therefore, if anyone is in Christ, he is a new creation; old things have passed away; behold, all things have become new."

2 Corinthians 5:17 (NKJV)

From Crawling Under Pews to Rising in Faith

Angela R. Edwards

Bio: Angela R. Edwards is a wife, mother, grandmother, and friend to many. As the owner of Pearly Gates Publishing and Redemption's Story Publishing, she has assisted numerous writers in realizing their dreams of becoming published authors since 2014. Angela is a prayer warrior, a domestic violence survivor, and the Trumpet for Change for others who have endured abuse through the Battle-Scar Free Movement. Her motto is, "Not today, Satan... and tomorrow isn't looking too good, either!"

Dedication: I dedicate my story to my mother, Marlowe R. Scott, for her many years of guidance on my spiritual journey. Thank you for keeping me grounded and focused on the Lord for all my needs, and thank you for being my friend. I love you!

MY PEWS

Hello, friends. My name is Angela Edwards [Boyce], and I am "Pew Baby." ☺ Let me explain. I was born and raised in a small town in New Jersey. From my birth until my early 20s, I attended Friendship A.M.E. (African Methodist Episcopal) Church. Although I don't remember doing it, I was told I used to crawl under the pews during church service, exploring every nook and cranny... along with the legs and feet of the congregants. As I understand it, everyone was quite understanding and tolerant of my antics, since I was the baby of the bunch at the time and loved by all.

As time went on and memories started to form, I remember spending every Sunday and holiday with my mother and siblings at Friendship. My mother, Marlowe, was very active in the church, serving as an usher and singing in the choir, among other duties. My brothers and I were expected to behave ourselves when she wasn't sitting in the pew beside us to keep us in line. (This was also at a time when "the village" helped raise and discipline children, so there was always someone within striking range when we acted up. I can recall a time or two when one of us was removed from the pew and given either a good talking-to or a spanking, depending on the offense.)

The pews were a sacred space in the church. Playing, wiggling, and talking were not tolerated for one second during the two-hour service. Imagine being an adventurous five-year-old who wanted nothing more than to do those things, no matter when! Fortunately, with my upbringing, I simply knew better and typically expended all that pent-up energy the instant my little feet stepped out the church's front door.

Let's fast-forward a few years to my early teens. I met and became best friends with a student named Carmen, who had moved from Maryland to New Jersey. Like me, she was the youngest of three, and we bonded almost instantly. One of my tasks was to invite Carmen to church. Her parents were hesitant at first because they practiced a different faith. Eventually, they allowed her to attend services with me, and our spiritual growth quickly became evident as we clung to each other and genuinely began to understand and embrace the pastor's teachings. I used to sing in the youth choir, which Carmen also joined after some time. Life was **GREAT**!

Around this same time, Friendship experienced a significant spiritual "revolution." The church I knew had become one of faith-filled, Holy Ghost-shouting people. That was something typically reserved for other churches, yet it somehow found its way into our congregation—and I was ready for it! This is a key part of my "pew" story. Keep reading...

When I was around 15, a guest pastor and his choir visited our church one evening for a revival service. Although I can't remember exactly where they came from, I do recall how their music and voices made me ***feel***. Every time they sang, my body would warm from the inside out. I couldn't quite put my finger on the feeling in that moment, but it was fantastic!

During that same service, Carmen and I sat at the back of the church in the last pew. It should be noted that several congregants were dancing and praising God throughout the service, especially when the choir was singing.

Well...

There we were—Carmen and I—in that back pew, giggling about how some of the praise worshippers were dancing. (Don't judge us; this was all relatively new to us at the time.) At some point, we stood, clapped, and sang along. Soon after, Carmen started mocking the worshippers, and we laughed and laughed. That was until... **SHE** caught the Holy Ghost for real! Instantly, I remembered Galatians 6:7, where it says, "...God is not mocked..." There she was, dancing and thrashing around in the pew—and I was initially alarmed. A few adults approached her but did not interrupt her praise. I remained planted in place, watching my bestie be overcome by the Spirit.

Dramatic pause... Wait for it... Wait for it...

The next thing I knew, I was getting up from the floor in the middle aisle.

From what I was ***told***, I simply praised and danced my way out of the pew—just like those whom Carmen and I mimicked. That was my first experience with the Holy Spirit. I'm blessed to say it wasn't my last. As I grew in my faith, I knew I wanted that closeness with God, and I understood it would come only by taking Him seriously. My playing around days in the pews were officially over! Singing His praises in the choir box took on a whole new meaning—not just for me, though. As more and more moments felt like Pentecost had fallen over the congregation, more youths experienced Him in new ways, and it was truly phenomenal!

One experience I pray I will never forget was when our youth choir visited a church in North Jersey, and an incredible event took place. We packed into the church van and a few cars with other adults to make the two-hour trip to perform at a gospel concert, and it was a stormy ride—literally. It poured rain from the moment we hit the turnpike (about 30 minutes into the trip). The choir that performed before us didn't engage the congregation at all, and it seemed the storm grew even worse as they sang. The thunderous booms and lightning flashes were intense!

When they finished, our choir climbed the steps and settled into the choir pews—sopranos, altos, and tenors in line—patiently waiting for the director to start playing the piano. About a minute into our set, the storm stopped, and the sun came out! The way the sunlight shone through the stained-glass windows was a breathtaking sight—and almost everyone noticed. What made the moment so special, you ask? Well, the first of two songs we sang was an upbeat version of "The Storm is Passing Over."

The original lyrics of the song were written by Charles A. Tindley in 1905. One of the stanzas reads like this:

"O billows rolling high, and thunder shakes the ground; the lightnings flash, and tempest all around. But Jesus walks on the sea and calms the angry waves, and the storm is passing over. Hallelujah!"

It was during the following refrain that the sun broke through the clouds and the rain stopped immediately:

"The storm is passing over! The storm is passing over! The storm is passing over! Hallelujah!"

Even as I recall the memory, I get chills from head to toe. I pray I did that part of my story justice and that, if you close your eyes and relive it with me, you'll join me in shouting, ***"THE STORM IS PASSING OVER! HALLELUJAH!"***

MY PERSPECTIVES

Growing up in the A.M.E. church was a blessing. There was structure in everything we did, with paper bifold programs handed out each Sunday to "back it up." From the moment we entered, we knew when service started, when the choir would march in, and what would happen during that two-hour period. The only time things might have gone awry (for the lack of a better word) was during the testimony part of the service, which was rare. Aside from that, the structure kept us grounded and prevented us from looking at our watches, **ESPECIALLY** during football season (for those of us who are fans of the game).

"Train up a child in the way he should go: and when he is old, he will not depart from it" (Proverbs 22:6).

After more than 20 years of faithful fellowship at Friendship, I finally left. Leadership had changed, many of my peers and I graduated high school and moved on to the next phase of life, and things just weren't the same anymore. My spirit was no longer being fed, and I became restless. My search led me to a couple of nondenominational churches, along with the man I was dating at the time. Even then, I was unfulfilled. Still, I knew I needed God in my life before I strayed too far, so I did my absolute best to find my footing. I also had two young children under my care and knew I was responsible for their spiritual growth.

Eventually, my soul found peace and stability at the church where my then-boyfriend's mother was a co-pastor. Much like Friendship was "back in the day," this church was spirit-filled. My children and I were welcomed with open arms, and I once again felt at home. While attending services there, congregants had the opportunity to attend Bible college under the guidance of none other than my boyfriend's mother, the co-pastor. I eagerly seized the chance to deepen my understanding of the Word! It also allowed me to gain a closer look at the woman who sat behind the pulpit. Did she walk the walk AND talk the talk? I am pleased to say that she did! The lessons I learned while attending Bible college were truly extraordinary. I'm an avid note-taker and still remember the lessons from those courses, referring to them now and then when I need clarity on a topic.

SIDEBAR: If you ever want to dive deeper into a Bible study and don't already own a comprehensive study guide, consider investing in "Willmington's Guide to the Bible," published by Tyndale House Publishers. It is a book designed for everyone, including (and I quote):

- "Pastors, attempting to provide for their preaching purposes a rapid, accurate, and workable outline analysis of those great scriptural facts they learned in college and seminary.
- Sunday school teachers, offering to them quick fingertip scriptural facts geared for effective teaching purposes.
- High school and college groups, presenting a "no-nonsense" historical, scientific, and theological summary of God's timeless Book for their uncertain age.
- Bible lovers everywhere, supporting their already-held convictions that the Bible is still the most exciting, practical, and inspirational Book ever written!"

Moving along...

I kept attending services at that church for almost seven years, leaving only after a painful breakup with my boyfriend. Even though there were many churches nearby, I wasn't attracted to any of them. Yes, I visited a few, but settling in wasn't easy for various reasons. Once again, I knew my spirit needed nourishment, so I kept searching unsuccessfully... for years.

I then met my husband, James, in 2005, and we got married in 2007. We left New Jersey and moved to Texas—an area completely unfamiliar to me. Fortunately, with the rise in internet use and popularity, finding a church home became easier. The first church I was drawn to was a megachurch in Houston, Texas. I absolutely **LOVED** the way the Holy Spirit moved there, but the "hometown fellowship" I longed for—the kind where people knew your name, and you could actually shake the pastor's hand—was missing. Still, I stayed there for about two years until I could no longer handle the disconnect from the congregation and leadership.

My search then led me to a smaller church, where I joined the praise team. Once again, I felt like I was in my element, and my soul was filled with joy. I fellowshipped with neighbors who also transplanted from the north to Texas. Our families got along well, which helped with the spiritual growth of all our children. (If it's not evident by now, making sure my children were rooted in the Word and knew and loved God was very important to me.) As a family, we attended that church for a few years until an unfortunate incident showed me it was time to move on. That incident involved my son and my friend's son. When we talked to the pastor about it, he downplayed its impact on **my** family and me, and I decided I could no longer remain under his leadership.

There are two words to describe what I felt at that moment: **CHURCH HURT.**

That was the first time in my life I had been directly affected by something like that, and I didn't know how to handle it in a positive way. So, what did I do? I walked away from the church entirely, unwilling to "risk" my spiritual health again—a stance I held for many years. I prayed at home. I studied at home. I worshipped with my family… at home.

It was *safe*. It was *fulfilling*. And it was ***lonely***.

Time went on, and then the COVID-19 pandemic hit hard. Churches switched to hosting online services, which made me excited all over again. The loneliness I had felt disappeared, and, as a community, we were all in the same space. Since there was no in-person fellowship, we all had to learn to embrace the "new normal" indefinitely. Most of us accepted this, although some simply couldn't get used to it. The online complaints in the church chats were so frequent that I sometimes muted the chat to focus on the service and sermon.

Anyway...

That became my "new normal." Even after the serious threat of the virus eased, I stayed at home, watching online services. I had grown comfortable, and my spirit was nourished weekly by the church I had connected with.

Let's fast forward a few years...

My children are now grown, each with their own families, leaving my husband and me as empty nesters. He retired from his job with the airlines, and we relocated to northeast Georgia. The search for a church home started again! After visiting a few, my son and his wife invited me to their church. When I say I ***LOVE*** it, that's an understatement! Every week, I look forward to the teachings. The pastor and his staff tag-team on sermon themes that last anywhere from two to six months. The praise and worship portion is truly phenomenal, and I see the fruits of my labor as I watch my son fellowship alongside his wife and their children. He is also actively involved with the men's group and often invites my husband to join him for a "men's night out."

Through it all, I am in awe of how God has never abandoned me. I am at home, my friend. I am at **HOME**! To God be the glory!

MY CONCLUSION

As I reflect on **MY** pews and **MY** perspectives, it's clear that the faith journey is just as much about the sacred spaces we inhabit as it is about the personal growth and transformation we experience within them. From the earliest days of crawling beneath the pews at Friendship A.M.E. Church to the profound spiritual awakenings that reshaped my worship and understanding, my story tells a testimony of discovery, resilience, and unwavering faith.

The pews, often considered just church furniture, symbolize much more than a place to sit. They represent sacred ground where discipline, reverence, and community intersect. As a child, the pews were initially a place of wonder. As I grew older, they became a space of structure and order, where playfulness was kept in check and respect for the service was of utmost importance. That early foundation fostered a deep sense of belonging and responsibility, shaped by the loving yet firm guidance of family and the broader church community. The discipline learned in those pews laid the groundwork for a faith that would later be tested and refined.

For as long as I can remember, the pews have also served as a stage for spiritual revolution and awakening. The shift from traditional worship to a livelier, Spirit-filled experience marked a pivotal point in my journey. The encounter with the Holy Spirit, first experienced in the back pews with my best friend, was truly transformative. It challenged my previous ideas of worship and opened the door to a more intimate, energetic relationship with God. That spiritual breakthrough shows how faith can grow, encouraging us to explore new ways to praise and connect with our Heavenly Father.

My story also highlights the importance of community and fellowship in nurturing faith. My participation in choirs, youth groups, and church events built bonds that strengthened my spiritual growth. The time when our choir performed during a storm, where the sun broke through the clouds at the exact moment of singing "The Storm is Passing Over," serves as a vivid metaphor for hope and divine intervention, reminding us that faith as small as a mustard seed can bring light in the darkest times.

However, my journey was not without its challenges. When I experienced "church hurt"—a painful moment when leadership failed to address a personal conflict—it highlighted that spiritual communities are made up of imperfect people. That hurt led to a period of withdrawal and solitary worship, reflecting a common struggle for many believers who face disappointment within their faith communities. Yet, even in isolation, my commitment to God stayed steadfast, showing that true faith can go beyond the walls of any building or the actions of any individual. The respect and admiration for the co-pastor who "walked the walk and talked the talk" sharply contrasted with the disappointment I felt when leadership failed to address my concerns. That contrast reminds us that spiritual leaders carry a profound responsibility to their congregations—not only to preach but to live the principles they teach. When that trust is broken, the impact can be deeply hurtful. Even then, healing and restoration are possible through continued faith and community support.

The shift to online worship during the COVID-19 pandemic marked a new chapter in my journey. While it fostered a sense of global community and accessibility, it also highlighted the evolving nature of fellowship and the challenges of staying connected in a virtual space. That period of adaptation further reinforced my faith's resilience and my ability to find spiritual nourishment in unexpected ways.

Faith, my friend, is a ***living***, ***breathing journey***—one that calls for flexibility, courage, and a heart open to God's movement in unexpected ways. We must be willing to step outside comfort zones, seek new expressions of worship, and stay connected even when we are physically apart.

Ultimately, I believe my story is one of hope and perseverance. It is a testament to the fact that no matter the trials, disappointments, or seasons of uncertainty, God's presence remains steadfast. The sacredness of the pews, once a place of childhood curiosity, then later, a sanctuary for profound spiritual encounters, symbolizes the constancy of God's invitation to come closer to Him, to worship Him, and to be transformed by Him.

I sincerely pray that something you've read here encourages you in your Christian faith, for you do not walk this journey alone. God bless, one and all!

A Prayer of Sacred Spaces and Faithful Journeys

Heavenly Father,

We come before You with hearts full of gratitude for the sacred spaces You have provided throughout our lives—the pews where we first learned to sit still in Your presence, the choir boxes where we lifted our voices to You in praise, and even the quiet corners of our homes where we have sought refuge when the church walls felt too confining or painful.

Lord, we thank You for the foundation of faith established in our early years. Like children crawling under the pews, exploring every corner with wonder and curiosity, we began our journey without fully understanding the enormity of Your love, yet surrounded by a community of believers who nurtured and protected us. We are grateful for the parents, ushers, choir members, and fellow believers who helped shape our understanding of what it means to belong to You. Thank You for the structure and discipline that taught us reverence, the traditions that grounded us, and the moments when Your Spirit broke through our expectations and transformed our worship into something vibrant and alive.

Father, we thank You for those unforgettable encounters with Your Holy Spirit—moments when we stopped mocking and began truly experiencing You, when we rose from the floor changed, and when the stormy weather stopped the very moment we sang of its passing. These divine encounters remind us that You are not distant or uninterested, but actively present, orchestrating moments of breakthrough that leave us breathless with wonder. Help us never to forget these sacred memories, and may they sustain us through seasons of doubt and lack.

We also bring before You the wounds we have borne: the church hurt that left us questioning whether we could ever trust again, the disappointments with leadership that caused us to retreat into isolation, and the times when those who should have shepherded us failed to see our pain. We acknowledge that Your church is made up of imperfect people, and we confess our own imperfections as well. Grant us the grace to forgive as we have been forgiven, and the wisdom to understand that our relationship with You surpasses any single building, denomination, or human leader.

Father, we ask for strength for those who are currently going through their own wilderness seasons as they worship alone, study in solitude, or long for community but are afraid to risk getting hurt again. Meet them in their homes, comfort them in their loneliness, and, when the time is right, lead them back to fellowship. Remind them that even in isolation, they are never truly alone, for You are Emmanuel, "God with us."

Guide us, Lord, as we continue this journey of faith. Help us stay flexible and open to new ways of worshipping, whether in traditional sanctuaries, megachurches, small congregations, or online communities. Teach us to recognize Your voice above the noise, follow Your guidance even when it leads us to unfamiliar places, and trust that You are always working to bring us home.

Finally, we pray for future generations—our children and grandchildren who observe how we handle faith's complexities. May our perseverance inspire them, our honesty about struggles encourage them to be genuine, and our unwavering trust in Your faithfulness guide them on the right path.

Thank You, Father, for never abandoning us. Thank You for being our constant through every season, storm, and transition. Like the sun breaking through the clouds at just the right moment, bless us on our paths and remind us that the storm is, indeed, passing over.

In Jesus' name we pray. Amen.

"Let your conduct be without covetousness; be content with such things as you have. For He Himself has said, 'I will never leave you nor forsake you.' So we may boldly say: 'The LORD is my helper; I will not fear. What can man do to me?'"

Hebrews 13:5-6 (NKJV)

"I have fought the good fight, I have finished the race, I have kept the faith. Finally, there is laid up for me the crown of righteousness, which the Lord, the righteous Judge, will give to me on that day, and not to me only but also to all who have loved His appearing."

2 Timothy 4:7-8 (NKJV)

From Ritual Religion to Real Relationship

Simone "Iman" Holyfield

Bio: Simone Holyfield, aka "Simone Iman," is an inspiring mother of three and a multi-talented, award-winning artist, singer, songwriter, producer, poet, author, and radio personality. She became a trailblazer as the first African-American artist to sign with Partridge Records, earning her the title "First Lady of Partridge Records." Her debut album, *Kismet*, released in 2009, marked the launch of her influential music career. Beyond her artistic achievements, Simone serves as the DEI Officer in Everett, Massachusetts, where she advocates for diversity and inclusion. Through the "Everett for Everyone" initiative, she empowers her community with cultural programs and celebrations that unite and uplift residents.

Dedication: This work is dedicated to God and to anyone who has ever felt lost in the Kingdom. May these words remind you that you are seen, known, loved, and called to a more intimate relationship with God, where hope is renewed, and your identity in Him remains secure.

I was born and raised in the church. For as long as I can remember, people have called me "Church Baby." In fact, my mommy still does. Some of my earliest memories are of sitting on the back pew while my grandmother (the head usher) stood at the front door, her presence both commanding and comforting. I recall how the choir's singing filled the sanctuary, towering above the faint murmur of prayers and the gentle hum of anticipation. The pastor's voice rose with inspiration, inviting the congregation to respond with a resounding "Amen!" Every Sunday morning felt like returning to a treasured ritual—one that wrapped me in its warmth and closeness. I would nestle between my grandmother and mother, their voices joining in prayer and praise while their steady hands held me in that sacred space. At any moment, if we children got fidgety or were too loud, a single glance from our elders was enough to restore reverent silence.

Church represented more than just a building to me; it felt like its own world. I remember being excited for Vacation Bible School, laughing and chatting with friends and cousins in Sunday school, and feeling the quiet during prayer meetings. As the seniors shared testimonies of faith and miracles, I listened and tried to envision a God who was close and all-powerful. But as I learned the lessons and studied the scriptures, the church—the walls, programs, and rituals—gradually became routine for me. I knew when to stand or sit and what to say, but I didn't truly grasp what it meant to know God personally.

For a long time, I only had the rituals... not a genuine relationship with God.

As I got older, church remained at the center of my life. My mother and grandmother were important members of the congregation, and I desired to follow their example and fit in. The church felt like a big family where we celebrated birthdays, shared meals, and supported each other through difficult times. I learned what "appropriate dress" meant for Sundays, memorized Bible verses, and bowed my head at the right moments. Still, beneath it all, I felt a quiet longing I couldn't explain. Something real was missing from my life.

I wanted to know God for myself, as if He were right there with me, but I kept going through the motions, hoping my faith would become real on its own. Maybe I liked the comfort of tradition or the feeling of community, so I didn't think much about the difference between **ritual** and ***relationship***. Church was what we did, and I was proud to do it well. I sang in the choir and helped out around the church. I could talk about God and share the stories, but deep down, I knew something was missing. Sometimes, after a powerful sermon or evening prayer, I wondered whether God even knew me or if I really knew Him. I tried not to dwell on those thoughts, believing that just showing up and behaving was enough.

My turning point didn't happen suddenly. In fact, it developed gradually—after two disappointing marriages, unanswered prayers, church hurts, and unmet hopes. During those times, I realized I was living on borrowed faith that belonged to my mother and grandmother, not my own. In moments of loss and heartbreak, when God felt distant, I clung even tighter to church routines, hoping the emptiness would fade. But it never did. Meanwhile, my longing for something genuine—something I could truly claim as my own—continued to grow. I wanted to know God *personally*, not just know *about* Him. I yearned to feel His presence, hear His voice, and experience the kind of relationship I witnessed others have with Him. That desire intensified year after year. I even explored Buddhism and New Age philosophies in my search for God. Ultimately, I couldn't ignore it any longer. It took 40 years after my baptism to truly find a relationship with God, which still surprises me.

Looking back, I realize I only knew about God and prayed to Him out of habit. Even though I saw God do incredible things over those 40 years and believed in the Holy Spirit, I didn't truly believe in God with all my heart. I didn't have a genuine relationship with Him. It was like being part of a club for God without really knowing Him. I used to think, "Once saved, always saved." Now I see I was definitely misled, but I can't blame anyone else. I was the one who deceived myself. Sure, I knew some scriptures and could talk about God with the best of them. Sometimes, I even said I was "catching the Holy Ghost," as if He were something I could catch like a cold. I thought I was fine, as long as I made it through the pearly gates of Heaven.

After 40 years, I was **done**.

I grew tired of living a life filled with defeat and shattered dreams, with no real sign of God, all because I had completely turned away from Him. I even dared to think I could have a blessed life without Him. A life without God stood out clearly, but I was the only one who thought I was okay. I had turned my back on Him and was doing everything except what He wanted, yet I still expected His blessings. It wasn't God who needed to change; I was the one who needed to obey. I just didn't know how.

Honestly, the only thing I knew to do was go back to the basics. I started praying more in a childlike way: when I talked to God, I imagined He was right there in front of me. I did that so often that I found myself talking to Him even while watching TV, asking for His thoughts. Whenever I faced a problem, I paused and included Him in the process. Soon, I felt Him encouraging me to read the Bible. I began at Genesis and read as if God were speaking directly to me. That made me feel special because I began to hear the Lord's voice in a new way. The words seemed to jump off the page and gave me real encouragement and answers.

What happened to me brought back memories of the time I took my daughter to Disney World years ago. She was so excited and only wanted to see Mickey Mouse and Tinker Bell. Her wish came true! She met Mickey, and by the end of the night, she saw Tinker Bell. I remember her waiting for Tinker during the fireworks show. We were in a huge crowd, but we managed to find the perfect spot, and Tinker flew right over our heads on a zipline. My daughter grabbed my arm and shouted, "Mommy, Tinker is real! She's really real!" I'll never forget that moment. That level of excitement matched how I felt when God finally showed up in my life in a big way.

For years, my life was filled with choir rehearsals, prayer meetings, Sunday school, and sermons—not just on Sundays, but all week long. What began as excitement became a habit. I memorized hymns before I truly understood worship and learned to raise my hands in praise, even though my heart was still searching for more. I continued the traditions because it made my family happy and helped me feel accepted. The church calendar was my calendar: Christmas, Easter, Convocation—each event marked time and my ongoing search for meaning. Yet, even with all those rituals, I never truly invited Christ into my heart.

During that critical time in my life, one scripture stayed with me: *"Only a fool says in his heart there is no God"* (Psalm 14:1). I had to admit: I was that fool. I practiced all the church rituals but had no real connection to God. That led me to leave Christianity and become a Buddhist. My church background made it easy for me to pray for long periods and give to the poor, so Buddhism felt like a natural fit... at first. In reality, it led me into more good works and a kind of spiritism I later regretted. I got involved in things I didn't understand until Christ delivered me.

Looking back now, I see that my search for God was also a search for myself. I tried to fill the emptiness with different philosophies, self-help books, and rituals that promised peace but only left me feeling emptier. My prayers became just words, and my worship felt automatic. Deep down, I wanted something real but kept settling for less.

The real change started when I hit my lowest point. I was truly broken and had lost all my pride. That's when I finally saw the truth: God was never far from me. I was the one who had wandered away.

One night, while alone in my room and afraid for both my daughter's life and my own because of the abuse we were enduring, I cried out to God—not out of habit, but out of desperation: "God, if You're real, I need You. Not another service, not another song, not another self-help book. I need You. I need You to save me for real!" That prayer changed everything. The answer didn't come in a flash of lightning or a sudden miracle; it came with a gentle stillness I had never felt before. I heard Him say, ***"Come home."*** For the first time, I felt God's presence around me and inside me.

Over the next two years, I learned to live out my faith one day at a time. Gradually, I began to understand what a true relationship with Christ meant. It wasn't about what I did for God, but about what He had done for me. Grace—unearned and unconditional—became real to me. All He desired was for me to spend time with Him and belong only to Him.

Since then, my journey hasn't been perfect. I still stumble, face doubts, and struggle with old habits. When doubt arises or I feel myself slipping, I try to pause and be honest with God about what I'm experiencing rather than hiding it. Prayer means everything to me now. I've learned that talking things through with God at every step makes life easier. I always turn to the Bible to see what He says about any situation. I know I can find a scripture that points me back to "What would Jesus do?" or what God wants for me. Those weak moments push me to lean on God, not run from Him. I now realize that I'm not alone. My faith isn't about obeying rules or trying to impress anyone. It's about getting up each day and saying, "God, I need You. Walk with me. Teach me. Change me," and then trusting Him to do it.

Scriptures began to feel more real to me in new ways. Verses I had memorized as a child finally started to make sense. *"Be still, and know that I am God"* (Psalm 46:10) remains my favorite verse. I've learned to listen quietly and trust as I wait. Another verse that empowers me is: *"My grace is always more than enough for you, and My power finds its full expression through your weakness"* (2 Corinthians 12:9, TPT Bible). Hallelujah! I stopped hiding my weaknesses and allowed God's strength to shine through them.

I found freedom when I let go. I stopped trying to control everything, earn God's love, or prove myself. Instead, I realize I am His beloved, chosen before the world began. If He loves me that much, I can trust Him with my fears, failures, and future. God's Word says that He has plans to give me "a hope and a future," and I choose to believe that.

As I write this, I think about many people who are still stuck in routines and longing for a genuine relationship with God. Maybe that's you. Maybe you've done everything right, but your heart still feels distant from Him. I want you to know He's closer than you realize. He's not waiting for you to fix yourself or be perfect; He desires you, just as you are. Spend time with Him in prayer. Come home.

If you're willing, take a simple step today. Just pause for a moment, wherever you are, and honestly talk to God. You might say, "God, I want to know You for real. Please help me take the next step toward You." Your conversation doesn't have to be perfect. Just start. Sometimes, that's all it takes to begin something new. Freedom, joy, and closeness await you when you surrender. Don't just go through the motions. Don't let another year pass by chasing shadows, as I did for so many years. Jesus said, *"I have come that they may have life, and have it to the full"* (John 10:10). That's what He wants for you: a real, abundant life full of meaning.

My story isn't unique. It's the story of every prodigal, every wanderer, and every child who has ever longed for home. The good news is that our Heavenly Father's arms are always open. No matter how far you've gone or how long you've been away, you can come home today... ***right now.***

So, I invite you to take off the mask. Release your burdens. Step out of routine and into a genuine relationship. Allow God to love you, heal you, and guide you into the abundant life He has prepared. You are not alone. You are seen, known, and loved more than you can imagine. God is your Father, Brother, and Best Friend. Let Him lead and direct you back to Himself. He is waiting for you.

A Prayer for Those Living on Borrowed Faith

Father God,

We come before You with honest hearts, acknowledging that it is possible to be born and raised in the church, be called "Church Baby," sit on pews for decades, and still not truly know You. We confess that we have sometimes confused religion with relationship, ritual with reality, and going through the motions with genuine devotion. Forgive us for the years we have lived on borrowed faith that belonged to our parents, grandparents, pastors, or church communities, but never became our own.

Lord, we thank You for the foundation that church traditions provide: Vacation Bible School laughter, Sunday school lessons, choir rehearsals, and prayer meetings. We are grateful for the grandmothers who stood as head ushers, commanding and comforting, and for the mothers whose voices joined in prayer and praise. We honor the elders who shared testimonies of faith and miracles and who gave us a single glance that restored reverent silence.

But Father, we also acknowledge the quiet longing that rituals alone cannot satisfy: the feeling that something real is missing, wondering whether You even know us or if we truly know You. We admit that sometimes we loved the comfort of tradition and the sense of community more than we sought intimacy with You. We have been proud to "do church well," sing in choirs, memorize scriptures, and bow our heads at the right moments, all while our hearts remained distant from Yours.

We lift up those who have spent years going through the motions, hoping their faith would become real on its own. We pray for those experiencing disappointing marriages, unanswered prayers, church hurts, and unmet hopes, who are realizing they have been living on borrowed faith. Meet them in their moments of loss and heartbreak. When You feel distant and they cling tighter to church routines, hoping the emptiness will fade, reveal to them that what they truly need is not more activity but more of You.

Father, we pray for those searching for You in all the wrong places: Buddhism, New Age philosophies, self-help books, and rituals that promise peace but leave them feeling emptier. We understand that their search for You is also a search for themselves, an attempt to fill a void that only You can satisfy. Bring them back home before they wander too far into spiritism and practices they will later regret. Deliver them and show them that You were never far from them; they were the ones who wandered away.

We thank You for the gift of hitting rock bottom, for the breaking that leads to a breakthrough. We praise You for the moments when all pride is lost, and truth becomes clear. Thank You for being found by those who cry out in desperation, "God, if You're real, I need You. Not another service. Not another song. Not another self-help book. I need You. I need You to save me for real!" Thank You for answering not with lightning or sudden miracles, but with gentle stillness and the words, "Come home."

Lord, we pray for those who are alone in their rooms right now, afraid for their lives or the lives of their children, enduring abuse and wondering if You see them. Hear their desperate cries. Surround them with Your presence at this moment, both around them and within them. Rescue them from danger and lead them to safety. Help them feel You in ways they have never experienced before.

We ask that You teach us what a true relationship with Christ means — that it's not about what we do for You, but about what You have done and will do for us. Help us understand grace as unearned and unconditional. All You desire is for us to spend time with You and belong only to You. Forgive us for trying to earn Your love, prove ourselves to You, or control everything. Help us realize we are Your beloved, chosen before the world began, and that You love us so much that we can trust You with our fears, failures, and future.

Father, we pray for those who will stumble, face doubts, and struggle with old habits. Teach them to pause and be honest with You about what they are experiencing rather than hiding it. Make prayer everything to them. Help them learn that talking things through with You at every step makes life easier. Lead them to Your Word so they can find scriptures that point them back to "What would Jesus do?" or what You want for them. In their weak moments, help them lean on You, not run from You.

We thank You for scriptures that become real in new ways—verses memorized in childhood that finally make sense in adulthood. Thank You for "Be still, and know that I am God" (Psalm 46:10), which teaches us to listen quietly and trust as we wait. Thank You for the promise that Your grace is always more than enough and that Your power finds its full expression through our weakness (2 Corinthians 12:9). Help us stop hiding our weaknesses and let Your strength shine through them.

Lord, we lift up everyone stuck in routines and longing for a genuine relationship with You. Speak to them clearly, letting them know You are closer than they realize. You are not waiting for them to fix themselves or be perfect; You desire them just as they are. Give them the courage to take a simple step today: pause wherever they are and honestly talk to You, saying, "God, I want to know You for real. Please help me take the next step toward You." We declare that their conversation doesn't have to be perfect; they just need to start.

Thank You, Father, that every prodigal's story, every wanderer's journey, and every child's longing for home ends the same way: with Your arms wide open. No matter how far we've gone or how long we've been away, we can come home today, right now. Thank You for waiting for us, pursuing us, and never giving up on us.

We are seen. We are known. We are loved more than we can imagine. You are our Father, Brother, and Best Friend. Lead and guide us back to You.

In Jesus' name, we pray. Amen.

"Because you have made the LORD, who is my refuge, even the Most High, your dwelling place, no evil shall befall you, nor shall any plague come near your dwelling; for He shall give His angels charge over you, to keep you in all your ways."

Psalm 91:9-11 (NKJV)

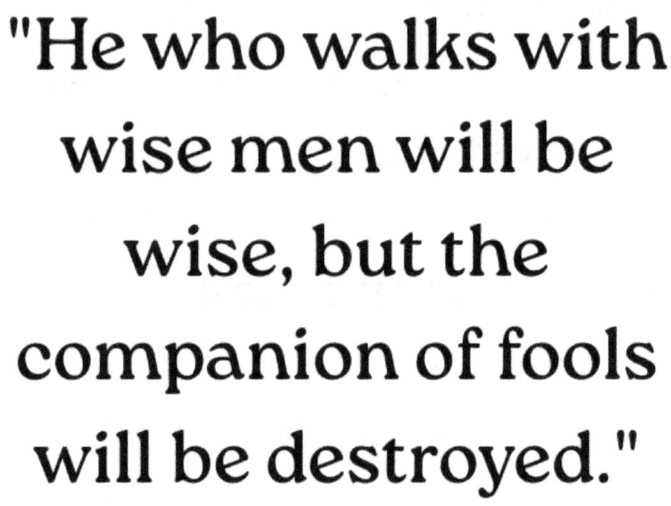

Proverbs 13:20 (NKJV)

Peppermints, Pews, and God's Plan

Min. Tosha R. Dearbone

Bio: Tosha Dearbone is a Christian Counselor, Author, and the Founder of Positive Express—a nonprofit empowering young girls and teens to recognize their worth and value. Born in Louisiana and raised in Houston, Texas, she is a mother, grandmother, and advocate with over 19 years of experience at Texas Children's Hospital. As a Medical Assistant, Certified Community Health Worker, Peer Recovery Coach, and Minister of the Gospel, Tosha dedicates her life to educating, uplifting, and inspiring others through faith and service. Connect with her at positive.express.14@gmail.com or 832-865-6582. Follow her on the web at www.positiveexpress.org.

Dedication: To those still sitting in the pews—watching, wondering, and quietly seeking God—this is for you. Even when you don't understand everything happening around you, God is still planting seeds. Your presence matters. Your questions matter. And, in His perfect time, those seeds will grow into a faith that is truly your own.

Looking back on my life, I see how seeds were being planted to help me develop my current relationship with God. I didn't realize it at the moment because I was just a young girl. The pews in my life held more than just people; they contained prayers, doubts, and unspoken cries to God. My faith was shaped not only by sermons and songs but also by moments of watching, waiting, and wondering. As my perspective changed, I understood that worship wasn't about where I sat, but about how open my heart was to God's presence.

I remember when I was a little girl, the day after my younger brother and I finished the school year, our mom would gas up the car and have us pack our bags for the summer to be shipped off to our grandmother's house—a four-and-a-half-hour drive to our hometown of Winnfield, Louisiana. As we pulled up to her house, we immediately knew Vacation Bible School at the gym was on the agenda. *(If you know, you know. LOL!)* We would get up every day and walk down Amos Street to the gym. On Sundays, we ended up at the church, sitting on pews with a bunch of strangers because "Madea" (that's what we called our grandmother) would be ushering, and we had no decision-making opportunities. So, we sat and watched the people around us whooping and hollering, clapping their hands, and shouting "Hallelujah!" We thought it was all kind of strange. After sitting there for what felt like hours and hours, we left no wiser than when we entered. We had no idea what the preacher talked about or why those people did all that "stuff."

Fast forward a few years...

Madea moved to Shreveport, Louisiana, after she got married. As we grew older, we started visiting her there, but we no longer attended church services. Not to mention, there was nothing to do except sit on the porch, peel peas, and feed the animals. (Well, ***they*** fed the animals because anyone who knows me knows that Tosha isn't touching or getting near anybody's animals!) Eventually, my brother and I got bored and asked if we could go stay with our aunt and cousins in our hometown. Madea let us go. What we didn't expect was being sent back to the gym and church. (I don't know why I thought things would be any different when my aunt was Madea's child. LOL!) You see, Madea's children knew that in order to stay in **her** house, "If you don't do anything else, you were going to serve the Lord!"—whether you understood what that meant or not. To know her, you would have loved her. So, as I sat in those pews, swinging my feet back and forth and eating peppermints to keep quiet, the seeds were being planted.

Fast forward a few more years...

I sometimes stayed over at my friend's house so we could go to the teen club called "Stadium Bowl." Stadium Bowl was a bowling alley with a dance club in the back. It was a hangout spot for teens to socialize, dance, and have fun. There was one catch, though: my friend's mother told us we could go to the party, but we had to wake up for church the next morning, and we agreed. Talk about being excited to go hang out! Plus, we were allowed to take her car, as long as we took care of it (LOL!). We made sure to do just that and even kept our promise to be home by curfew. Sunday morning sure came quickly!

As promised, we woke up early to prepare for service at Windsor Village Methodist Church. I remember walking in and hearing the music playing before taking my friend's little brother to the children's building and then returning to the main sanctuary to sit with her mom. The church was packed with people, including many in the balconies, while we sat down low. Once again, I saw people standing with their hands in the air and doing "stuff," while others remained sitting on the pews, and I still didn't understand the preacher's message. When I went to church with my grandmother and aunt in those earlier years, nothing was explained about what happened in the church.

One Sunday, as we were getting ready to leave, I remember touching my chest and feeling something I had never experienced before: my body was warm, and I felt happy. I didn't share that with anyone because I didn't want to seem "crazy." I just knew it was something new and unfamiliar. From that day on, Sunday after Sunday, I felt that warm sensation flow through my entire body.

A year or so passed, and I started visiting another friend's church, "Morning Star," with her and her grandmother. Although that church was smaller, it still made an impact on me. It left a mark in such a way that when I received my first car at 16, I no longer needed to ride with them to church, so I drove myself there. At that point, I began to learn more about the man they called Jesus. I took notes while sitting on the pews, sang along with the congregation, and looked up certain scriptures I heard. That began a new journey for me. No longer was it just Sunday mornings; I started seeking God during the midweek services, too. I sat underneath that ministry off and on for about nine years.

Then, in 2015, I saw a woman on Facebook hosting a webinar on self-esteem. The woman was Pastor Peters, Founder of Women of Divine Distinction. I attended the webinar and kept in touch with her over the years. I remember she used to host 24-hour prayer calls, especially around Easter. The calls involved dialing into a prayer line to hear different preachers and teachers share a word and, of course, pray. I will never forget the day she called my name to pray during one of those calls. Thank God it wasn't a Zoom call, because my face showed everything except "equipped." I didn't feel prepared, let alone qualified, to pray out loud. In fact, I started squirming and sweating profusely. Nonetheless, I pushed past my nervousness and began to pray. To me, it wasn't a strong prayer. All I could think of was what a coach once told me: "Do it afraid"—and that's what I did. When that call ended, I felt like I had made a fool of myself, but Pastor Peters assured me I had done well. So, from time to time, Pastor Peters asked me to pray, and even though it still felt hard, I persevered.

I remember a Friday when a pastor during a call caught my attention. His message began to speak to me in ways I couldn't understand, but I knew I wanted more of what he was talking about. He mentioned starting a church with his wife, so when the timing felt right, I drove to the north side of Houston, Texas, to visit. Without clear guidance from the Lord, I quickly joined his church. I recall those times when very few people attended services, mostly family members and grandparents, one of whom was the other pastor of the church.

Weeks went by. I remained a faithful member, making church attendance part of my Sunday drive across Houston. Being the only member outside their family felt strange, but God's Word was shared and always seemed relevant to my life at that time. Eventually, my children began attending with me. My son, Chris, and my nephew began following the pastor and his messages, which I truly yearned for. I hoped my children would develop their own relationship with Christ so it wouldn't feel forced. It was important to me that they used their own free will and understood for themselves, so much so that when we agreed to be baptized, my daughter, Treasure, did as well. Talk about a happy mother! After our baptism, I started to see a change in her, but that was short-lived due to the world's influence, and she began to backslide. Still, I kept praying because I knew "once saved, always saved." Plus, I believed that with God, He could turn things around.

Some time passed, and I began to experience what most people call "church hurt." I started to sense that something was "off" with the First Lady of the church. Her change in behavior toward me became apparent. At first, I tried to dismiss the feeling, but it grew stronger. My spirit was torn between my emotions and my discernment of what was actually happening. One day, I reached out to the pastor but received no response. Then, I contacted the First Lady, only to get a text message back that seemed like pushback and flesh-driven. That's right: **flesh-driven**! It ignited something inside me that told me to stop going, which I did after the pastor never responded to my concerns.

For a while, I sat still, awaiting instructions from the Lord. In the interim, I watched The Potter House services online with Bishop T.D. Jakes and his daughter, Pastor Sarah Jakes. Then, one day, as I was scrolling through Facebook, I stumbled upon a familiar face. It stopped me in my tracks, and I was soon going down a rabbit hole, listening to that man's different sermons. I remember thinking, "Wow! He used to be a Confidence Coach on Periscope (an online chat system that allowed people to go live and send messages to others)!" I got excited and scrolled through some of his sermons. Soon, I thought, "I am going to visit his church."

A couple of weeks later, I gathered the courage to visit. It turned out the church wasn't too far from where I lived at the time. As I walked in, I felt love and calmness in the atmosphere, which brought my soul peace. Everyone was so polite and welcoming throughout the service. They performed an act of kindness called "Love and Hugs," where everyone would go around hugging each other and greeting new visitors. Coming from a childhood where hugging was rare, I can't quite explain how I felt, but it grew on me. I remember when the pastor came around and saw me, he greeted me by name: "Welcome, Tosha

Dearbone!" I was surprised because I couldn't figure out how he knew my name! My ID on Periscope wasn't my real name; it was my nonprofit organization's name, "Positive Express." Maybe he had the time and looked up his followers who frequently interacted. I simply don't know...

After the service, I briefly spoke with the pastor and his wife. I was asked, "How was the service?" I replied, "It was good. I'll be back, not just as a visitor. I'll more than likely join." A couple of Sundays went by, and I decided to return. The spirit was high as I entered the sanctuary, and when the pastor asked about making this our church home, my hand went up. I had decided in my mind that this was the place God said to call "home."

Immediately, I shifted into servant mode, serving as a greeter at the front door and then as a teacher in the children's ministry. I always knew I would do something with the youth. At the time, the church didn't have a team director or leader, so another woman and I were pretty much winging it and doing what we believed was right—and it worked! Then, one day during the COVID pandemic, we were introduced to the new Youth Director. The other woman and I were left speechless because even with the director there, we were still doing all the work. She even told us she would provide us with the curriculum, activities, etc., but that never happened. Something had to be done, so we asked to meet with the leaders to discuss what was going on and describe how chaotic things were becoming. After all, if that woman was hired to do a job, but we were the ones doing all the work, why was she there? Yes, the leaders listened, but they believed she was a good fit, so we let it go. Then, after calling many times and saying she wasn't coming into work, the new director was suddenly gone. That made sense to us because we didn't need someone who wasn't going to put forth the effort to do the job anyway!

A short time later, our space in the building was being sold, and we transitioned to online services until we could find a new location. That arrangement worked for us because we could still receive the Word online and attend ministerial training classes (I believe it was called something else, but I can't recall the exact name). Then, in 2024, we began holding services at the Power Center in Houston, Texas. In August 2024, I received a call about an open position to become the Youth Director, and since my focus was on serving the youth, I immediately accepted. I was excited to review the curriculum and do what I knew God had gifted me to do. Each Sunday, some leaders and volunteers would meet at the church to set up and prepare for the day. Was it a lot of work? Yes, but it was worth it. I always obeyed and did whatever needed to be done without complaint.

Let's now look at 2025 and beyond. I was ordained as a Minister of the Gospel. Even then, it didn't feel genuine. Far too often, things changed quickly within the church to the point that I started to feel overlooked, overwhelmed, and unworthy of certain relationships. I saw my leaders take the stance of, "If you don't fit a certain image or have a certain income, then you are not our people," but I stayed quiet and remained humble because I honored them. Did I get frustrated often? Absolutely, because I knew it was out of character for them... or so I thought.

One day, I decided to become more involved in their faith circles—not just participate but also take on a leadership role. I ended up serving as a regional leader for my faith circle and another one. Things were going smoothly, and the women were enjoying the experience. That was until...

I received a text message asking whose group a specific member was in. I was about to respond, "Who is that?" before realizing which circle she belonged to. I called the Human Resources (HR) person and told her about the message, but she gave me an earful instead. She asked how I could entertain the conversation instead of stopping it, especially since it involved our leader. I quickly replied, "I wasn't even there, but let me find out who was and what was said." I called the circle leaders one by one, but no one answered. A few minutes later, I received a text from one of them with four names. I called the HR woman back and explained the message. She then told me who she believed had stirred the pot and why. Wow! After all that, I got the response that she was upset because they were talking about her baby.

Amid all that, drama filled the airwaves and rumors started to spread. It affected me because it became overwhelming. One person ended up in the hospital, and another still wanted some type of face-to-face meeting, but that was shut down and dismissed as if it wasn't the right decision.

One day, I kept hearing the Holy Spirit tell me it was time for a shift—something that had been prophesied to me over a month earlier. Due to all the calls and false rumors continuing to spread, I realized it was time to resign from the church. I emailed the leaders and shared how I felt. Immediately, the executive pastor called me to ask what was going on. As I explained, he said, "I can see that." Then I received a call from the pastor. Meanwhile, the executive pastor was texting me, instructing me to tell everything, which I did. The pastor asked me to write down everything we discussed and to allow him and his wife to set up a meeting to address the issues. I agreed. Then his wife called, shared her feelings, and said she hadn't heard about any of what I mentioned. *Hmm... I didn't believe* ***that***. Many others called me as well, asking about what happened, but I refused to participate in any more of the foolishness, so those calls were cut short.

Days passed, and I attended the Five-Fold Ministry training. As I sat there, I sensed an opposing spirit in the room. I tried to ignore it, but it weighed heavily on my spirit. The next day was a Wednesday, and before I could fully exit the car and enter the church, I spoke to the Holy Spirit, saying, "If the message tonight has anything to do with what has been happening, I am done." Now, mind you, up to that point, no meeting had been scheduled. When I entered, the pastor and another leader were standing just inside the doorway. We exchanged greetings before I walked into the sanctuary and took a seat. That day, I sat in a different spot and took out my paper and pen. As soon as the speaker opened her mouth, the Holy Spirit began to reveal the flesh behind her message. I knew what needed to be done. It was time for me to go. I was hurt and confused. How was it possible for all that mess to be turned on me? I was also torn because someone I looked up to had publicly aired out the offenses without any thought given to how I and others would see that mean-girl spirit take over.

The very next day, I woke up and submitted my final resignation letter with tears in my eyes. For nine years, I was a loyal and faithful servant. I truly honored my leaders, even though I felt unloved and unsupported, unlike others. I received an email reply from the pastor's wife, and, of course, no accountability for her actions was given. Instead, I received a slew of excuses and accusatory undertones, attempting to make me think I had done something wrong.

As I conclude my *Pews & Perspectives* story, I must share that although many are still calling and questioning my decision, what surprises me the most are the ones who text and say, "There is a conflict of interest," and that they must stop interacting with me. I truly never saw ***that*** coming. Am I hurt? Yes, but I'd rather be obedient to the Lord than remain somewhere where I'm not valued. No meeting. No accountability. Disrespected. Cast out. I am done.

My prayer today is that God heals the wounded parts of me, as only He can.

A Prayer for the Wounded and Faithful

Heavenly Father,

We come before You with hearts that have been broken by the very places meant to nurture them. We lift up those who have served faithfully for years, only to find themselves disrespected, cast out, and questioning whether their loyalty and love ever truly mattered. Lord, You see every tear shed in confusion and pain. You know the hurt of being valued for what we can do for others rather than for who we are in You.

Thank You, Father, for planting seeds in us long before we understood what was growing. We are grateful for the grandmothers who made sure we went to church whether we understood it or not, and for the pews where we sat, swinging our feet and eating peppermints, while Your Word was being sown into our young hearts. We didn't know it then, but You were preparing, shaping, and drawing us closer even when the sermons made no sense and the "whooping and hollering" seemed strange. Thank You for being patient with our confusion and for never giving up on us, even when we had no idea what was happening.

We praise You for those warm feelings that flow through our bodies—those unexplainable moments when we touch our chests and sense something we've never felt before. Thank You for revealing Yourself to us in ways that are personal and undeniable, and for those times when happiness and warmth flood our souls, and we know, without a doubt, that You are real and near.

Lord, we are thankful for the journey from watching to participating, from wondering to seeking, and from sitting in pews as strangers to driving ourselves to church because we truly wanted to learn about the man called Jesus. Thank You for the growth of our faith, midweek services that deepened our hunger, notes taken during sermons, and scriptures we looked up ourselves. Thank You for calling us to pray even when we felt unequipped and unprepared, and for the courage to overcome our nervousness and obey.

We lift up those who have experienced church hurt in its most painful forms—the ones who served as greeters, teachers, youth directors, and ministers, only to be overlooked, overwhelmed, and made to feel unworthy. Father, comfort those who have witnessed mean-girl spirits take over leadership, have been caught in the crossfire of drama and false rumors, and have been told there is a "conflict of interest" so the relationships must end simply because they chose obedience over comfort. Heal the wounded parts of them that only You can heal.

We pray for those who have heard Your voice say, "It's time for a shift," even when it meant walking away from years of faithful service, cherished positions, and the communities they called home. Give them the strength to trust Your guidance even when it doesn't make sense, no accountability is provided, and no apology is made. Remind them that their worth is not determined by how church leaders treat them, but by how You see them: beloved, worthy, and precious.

Father, we ask for discernment for those still sitting in pews, watching and wondering. Help them recognize when the Holy Spirit is revealing flesh behind messages, when opposing spirits fill the rooms, when it's time to stay, and when it's time to go. Give them the courage to submit their resignation letters with tears in their eyes if that's what obedience requires, knowing that You will never leave them without a home.

We pray for healing from the pain of being treated as "not our people" because of image or income, the sting of being accused when we were the ones wronged, and the confusion of watching those we honored fail to honor us in return. Lord, replace bitterness with peace, resentment with grace, and hurt with hope. Help us forgive even when no apology comes, and to release those who have chosen to stop interacting with us.

Thank You for the prophecies spoken over our lives that prepare us for shifts before they happen. Thank You for being our constant when church communities fail us, for being our home when we must leave buildings behind, and for being our validation when leaders make us feel invisible.

We declare that we would rather be obedient to You than stay somewhere we are not appreciated. We choose to honor You above everything, serve You faithfully even when earthly recognition never comes, and trust that You are guiding our steps toward something better.

Heal us, Lord. Restore us. And lead us to communities where love is genuine, service is appreciated, and Your presence is truly the focus.

In Jesus' name, we pray. Amen.

"And we know that all things work together for good to those who love God, to those who are called according to His purpose."

Romans 8:28 (NKJV)

"Brethren, I do not count myself to have apprehended; but one thing I do, forgetting those things which are behind and reaching forward to those things which are ahead, I press toward the goal for the prize of the upward call of God in Christ Jesus."

Philippians 3:13-14 (NKJV)

My Faith! My Faith! My Faith!

Reyna Harris-Goynes

Bio: Reyna Harris-Goynes is a wife, mother of five, and owner of V.R. Fashions & More and V.R. Mobile Notary. She is also a bestselling author who has contributed to more than 15 anthologies during her literary career. Reyna states, “I love being a business owner and customizing items for my customers!”

Dedication: I dedicate my story to my husband, Victor Goynes, because without him in my life, I don’t know where my FAITH in GOD would’ve taken me. When I wanted to give up on life, Victor said no—and so did God. My husband was definitely meant to be in my life.

Have you ever faced a situation where God tested your faith? I definitely have—more than once. One specific moment stands out when I almost lost my life...

At the time, I was at home with some friends. A couple of guys were standing behind me near my deep freezer, messing with a gun. Suddenly, the gun went off behind me. The bullet whizzed past my head and hit a guy just as he was about to step outside my apartment. If I had still been leaning to the side, the bullet would have hit me in the head. Instead, it hit the guy in the front of his leg, went out the back, went through the front of my television, out the back, and finally lodged into the wall.

I thought I was going to lose my mind, not just because there was blood everywhere, but especially after the police put my best friend in the back of the police car because they thought he was involved in the incident. He wasn't. The guy who the gun belonged to took off before the police arrived. He didn't even so much as apologize for the damage done to my friend and my apartment. The other guy apologized the next day and added, "How can I explain what happened to your kids?"

I cleaned up the blood while the police officers talked to my best friend and the guy who got shot in the leg. All the while, my mind raced a hundred miles an hour. All I could think was, "What if that bullet had hit me in the back of my head while my children slept in the bedroom?" Fortunately, they were sleeping so deeply that they slept through all the commotion in the apartment, including the gunshot and the police arriving with their guns drawn and pointed at my neighbor and me.

As expected, the police completed their investigation of the scene and finished all the paperwork. After they left, I couldn't help but wonder why that incident even happened, especially since I had told the guys to stop playing with the gun in the first place. That was truly a wake-up call that taught me a lot about people and their lack of respect for me and *themselves* in this world.

Perhaps the greatest lesson I learned that night was that God is truly who He says He is and always has been: a FATHER. I was so traumatized afterward, unsure how I could move past almost being killed and leaving my children motherless because of someone else's careless actions. For a long time, all I could think about was "What if?" After all, I never saw it coming. That was the first time I ever saw my life flash before my eyes. I'm grateful for God's hands being all over that entire situation.

God saw fit for me to keep living for my children at that time, and I thank Him every day for what He has done for me. He has blessed me in ways I never expected, including bringing my husband back into my life after all my trials and tribulations. Only God knows why things happen and when they will happen in this thing called "life."

Although I understand that people make mistakes, I can't help but think that the shooting wasn't one. I believe God was telling me to change the people I socialize with from that point on. In fact, ever since I stopped associating with certain people, many things have improved for me in a positive way. Since I didn't like the way things were going in my life, God whispered, "Change it, and change your company so you can do better."

Here's what I'd like to share with you, and the message is plain and simple: No matter what God takes you through—no matter how He tests your faith—make the best of it. Take things one day at a time, always.

Amid everything I was going through then and even now, I've never lost my FAITH or HOPE in GOD. When no one else is around, I know He is always with me, day and night. I didn't realize back then just how much I needed God, but I'm not ashamed to admit that I need Him now, more than ever. He is truly a right-on-time GOD!

****

Editor's Note: Bearing Witness to Divine Intervention

In "My Faith! My Faith! My Faith!" Reyna Harris-Goynes offers a testimony that captures the intersection of urban life and spiritual awakening—a story that refuses to sugarcoat life's chaos while revealing the unseen hand of providence at work. This isn't a tale for those looking for easy answers about faith. Instead, it's a raw, honest account of how near-death experiences can spark profound transformation.

The story quickly pulls readers into a domestic scene that suddenly erupts into violence. What begins as an ordinary evening—friends gathered, everyday home life—shatters in an instant when a gun fires. The path of the bullet, carefully tracked by Reyna, becomes a visual proof of divine protection: past her head, through a man's leg, through a television, into a wall. Each point along this route shows a potential fatality avoided, a life saved by what the author attributes to inches and the hand of God.

The power of this account lies not only in its dramatic centerpiece but also in the circles of consequence that ripple outward from that single gunshot. Reyna skillfully layers the immediate chaos—blood, police, drawn weapons—along with the deeper psychological aftermath. Her children slept through the entire ordeal, a detail that amplifies rather than diminishes the horror. Her mind races with counterfactuals: What if the bullet had found her? What if her children had awakened to witness their mother's death? Those questions turn a personal near-miss into a reflection on maternal responsibility and the fragility of the family unit.

Particularly compelling is Reyna's approach to accountability and absence. The gun's owner leaves without an apology, a detail that reveals a culture of recklessness and moral neglect within her social circle at that time. That abandonment—both physical and moral—acts as a catalyst for Reyna's eventual confrontation with the company she keeps. The story then becomes a lesson in discernment, showing how crises can heighten our awareness of who truly deserves access to our lives and the safety of our children.

The transformation arc Reyna traces is neither quick nor simple. She doesn't claim instant enlightenment but describes a long process of trauma, obsessive "What if?" thoughts, and a gradual understanding. This realism keeps the spiritual testimony rooted in the human experience. The reader sees not a sudden conversion but a slow awakening to patterns that no longer help her—a realization that God's protection at that moment was also an invitation to take part in her own deliverance by making different choices.

Reyna writes from a position of hard-won wisdom, speaking to readers who might find themselves in similarly risky situations or relationships. Her target audience appears to be those who, like her former self, may not fully recognize dangers lurking in their social circles or realize how much they need God's divine guidance. Her straightforward writing style shows she understands her readers' need for clarity rather than complexity. Some may need permission to make difficult changes and reassurance that faith can remain strong even when tested by violence and betrayal.

What sets this testimony apart from typical faith stories is its refusal to diminish human effort. Yes, God protected her—

but she also had to clean up the blood, work through the trauma, and make the tough choice to cut ties with those who threatened her and her children's lives. The divine and the human work together in her salvation, each affirming the other's role.

The story's importance goes beyond personal testimony and serves as social commentary. It highlights the specific vulnerabilities faced by those in communities where gun violence breaks into domestic spaces, where police show up with weapons drawn, and where the wrong company can cost you everything. Reyna turns her near-death experience into a warning and a guide for others trying to escape similar situations.

As you reflect on her testimony, consider this: What relationships in your own life exist on borrowed time, and what will it take for you to recognize that God's protection is also a call to action?

A Prayer of Protection and Transformation

Heavenly Father,

We come before You with hearts full of gratitude for Your divine protection—the kind that defies logic and explanation, the kind that measures itself in inches between life and death. Thank You for being the God who sees danger before it fully manifests, who positions us just out of harm's way, and who redirects bullets and alters trajectories in ways we cannot comprehend until we look back and trace the path of what could have been.

Lord, we thank You for the night You saved a mother's life while her children slept peacefully in the next room, unaware that their world nearly shattered. We praise You for being the shield that stood between a careless gunshot and a fatal outcome, and for being the invisible hand that moved a head just enough, preventing a bullet from hitting its mark. We acknowledge that You are the God of inches and seconds, of split-second interventions that change everything.

Father, we lift up every person who has ever stood in the aftermath of violence as they cleaned up blood while their minds raced, replaying the "what ifs" that haunt their nights and steal their peace. Comfort those who have seen their lives flash before their eyes, carry the trauma of near-misses, and cannot stop thinking about how differently things could have ended. Remind them that You were present in that moment, that Your protection was real, and that their survival has a purpose.

We pray for those who have had to confront the painful reality that some people in their lives do not respect them or their homes, and who bring chaos and danger into sacred spaces where children should be safe. Give them the courage to recognize toxic relationships for what they are, the strength to cut ties that need to be severed, and the wisdom to discern who truly deserves access to their lives and families. Help them hear You whisper, "Change it. Change your company so you can do better."

Lord, we recognize that making these changes is difficult. It involves confronting our own patterns, admitting we've tolerated what should not have been, and sometimes walking away from people we've known for years. Grant courage to those facing tough decisions about friendships, social circles, and the company they keep. Protect them from guilt, the pressure to hold on to harmful relationships, and the fear of being alone. Remind them that when they remove toxic people from their lives, You will fill those spaces with something better.

We thank You, Father, for being a right-on-time God. Not early, not late, but always exactly when we need You most. Thank You for the moments when no one else is around, but You are there—day and night—never leaving or forsaking. Thank You for being the Father who sees beyond our immediate circumstances to the purpose You have for our lives.

We pray for parents everywhere who carry the weight of protecting their children, who lie awake at night thinking about all the dangers they cannot control, and who blame themselves for situations that were never their fault. Release them from the "what if" burden. Help them trust that just as You protected them once, You will continue to be their refuge and fortress. Grant them peace that surpasses understanding, the kind that allows them to sleep soundly knowing their children are covered by Your hand.

Father, we lift up those who have been traumatized by gun violence, whether they were directly harmed, witnessed shootings, or narrowly escaped with their lives. Heal the psychological wounds that bullets leave behind—the hypervigilance, flashbacks, and inability to feel safe in their own homes. Restore their sense of security and remind them that You are their dwelling place, and that no evil shall ultimately befall those who make You their refuge.

We pray for communities where gun violence is not an anomaly but a regular occurrence, where police arrive with weapons drawn, where children learn to sleep through gunshots, and where cleaning blood from the floor happens all too often. Bring transformation to those communities, Lord. Raise up leaders who will address root causes, provide alternatives to violence, and create environments where families can thrive without fear.

Thank You, God, for the gift of second chances and for allowing us to survive what should have ended us so we can live differently, love more fully, and testify to Your goodness. Thank You for the trials that test our faith, not to break us but to shape us, to show us what we are made of and reveal who You are amid the chaos.

Helps us all to take things one day at a time, make the best of what You lead us through, and never lose our faith or hope in You. May we recognize that Your protection is also a call to action, to change what needs changing, to walk away from what threatens us, and to walk toward the abundant life You have prepared.

Finally, Lord, we pray for everyone who sees themselves in Reyna's testimony—those who have faced situations where their faith was tested, survived what should have broken them, and are still processing trauma and trying to understand why they are still here. Speak to them clearly: "You are still here because I have a purpose for your life. You survived because your story is not finished. You were protected because your spouse, children, community, and future still need you."

We declare that You are who You say You are and always have been: a Father, protector, and right-on-time God who blesses us in ways we do not deserve or expect.

In Jesus' mighty name, we pray. Amen.

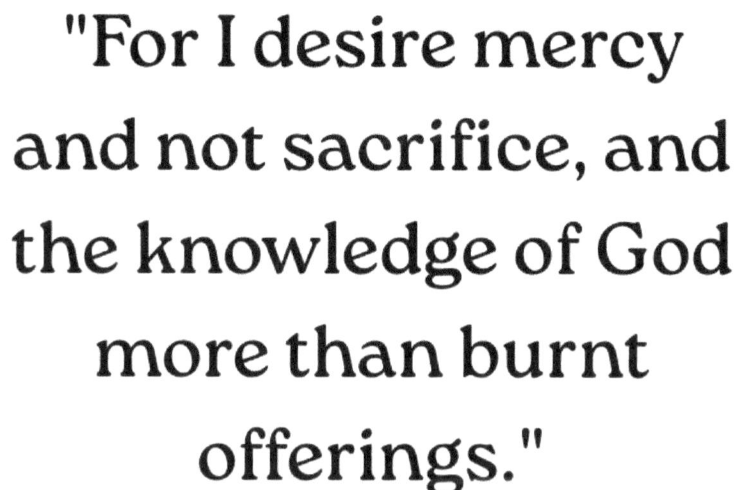

"For I desire mercy and not sacrifice, and the knowledge of God more than burnt offerings."

Hosea 6:6 (NKJV)

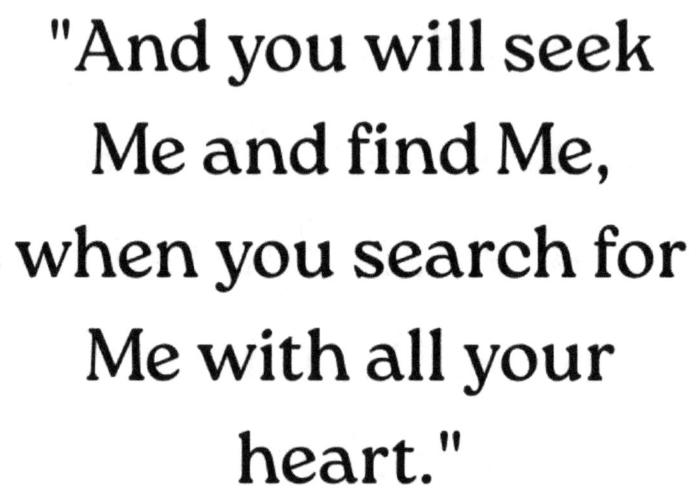

"And you will seek Me and find Me, when you search for Me with all your heart."

Jeremiah 29:13 (NKJV)

Conclusion

My friends, we have journeyed together through decades of worship experiences, from the 1940s to the present day, across geographic boundaries and denominational lines, through moments of profound spiritual awakening and seasons of devastating church hurt. We have sat in pews with a curious child crawling beneath them, stood in aisles with a man whose feet felt like cement as he answered God's call, watched storms literally cease as youth choirs sang of their passing, and witnessed faithful servants walk away from communities they loved because obedience to God required it. These stories have been gifts—honest, raw, and redemptive testimonies of what it means to pursue faith in the context of imperfect communities led by imperfect people.

As we conclude this collection, it is worth reflecting on what these narratives collectively teach us about the nature of faith, the purpose of the church, and God's character. These are not merely individual stories; they form a connection that reveals universal truths about the Christian journey. They're truths that transcend time, place, and circumstance.

One of the most profound lessons in these testimonies is that faith operates on two levels simultaneously: it is both a gift from God and a choice we make repeatedly throughout our lives. We see faith planted in the seeds long before understanding its bloom.

A grandmother insisted that her grandchildren attend Vacation Bible School and church services, even when they had "no decision-making opportunities."

A mother faithfully served as an usher and choir member, demonstrating the value of devotion to her children.

A friend invited another to church, and their spiritual growth became evident as they clung to each other and embraced the pastor's teachings.

Each was a moment of divine initiative: God planted, pursued, called, and transformed.

But we also see the choice aspect in every story: the decision to drive to church at 16 because of a genuine desire to learn about Jesus, the commitment to keep searching for a spiritual home even after years of disappointment, and the perseverance to stay faithful for over 80 years despite being turned away, dismissed, and disrespected.

These stories teach us that faith is a partnership between the divine and the human. God takes the first step, but we must respond. God plants seeds, but we must water them and nurture growth. God calls us, but we must answer. God provides grace, but we must choose to walk in it every day. This understanding frees us from two dangerous extremes: the passivity that says, "If God wants it to happen, it will," and the pride that claims, "My faith is entirely my own achievement." Faith is both a gift and a choice, grace and effort, divine sovereignty and human responsibility working together in a mysterious harmony.

These stories also challenge us to confront the dual nature of the church. It is both where we meet God most deeply and where we endure some of our greatest wounds.

The church as a sanctuary is beautifully depicted in these pages. It appears when the Holy Spirit falls on two teenage girls in the back pew, transforming mockery into sincere worship. It is felt in the sacred waters of baptism, where old lives fade away, and new creations arise. We rejoice in the multigenerational worship service where grandparents, parents, and children stand side by side, passing faith from one generation to the next.

But the church as a battleground remains equally present. We see it in the public humiliation of a faithful choir member who missed one rehearsal and was denied the chance to worship with others. We observe it in the pastor who ignores reports of financial misconduct and never responds to legitimate concerns. We experience it through the drama, false rumors, and mean-spirited attitudes that infiltrate leadership and poison the community.

In our humanness, we might be tempted to pick sides when faced with that dual reality. Do we idealize the church and deny its capacity for harm, or do we demonize it and walk away altogether? The storytellers in this book show a third way: they hold the tension. They love the church while recognizing its brokenness. They respect spiritual leaders but also see when those leaders fail. They stay committed to the body of Christ while protecting themselves from toxic environments. They understand that the church is not the fully realized Kingdom of God but a community of broken people being gradually transformed by a perfect God.

Those perspectives enable them to leave churches when necessary without abandoning their faith, to critique leadership without becoming cynical, and to protect their spiritual well-being without abandoning the call to community. It is a mature faith that can say, "I have been deeply hurt by the church, but I still believe in the church. I have been failed by leaders, but I still honor godly leadership. I have experienced the worst of Christian community, but I still long for its best."

Another consistent theme across these testimonies is that spiritual growth often requires us to let go of what we've been holding onto: positions, relationships, communities, and even our own understanding of how things should be. Moments of release are rarely easy. They usually involve grief, confusion, and the fear of making the wrong choice. But they also demonstrate a deep trust in God's guidance. Sometimes, the most faithful action is to walk away from what feels comfortable, respected, or expected to follow where God leads. They show us that loyalty to God must take precedence over loyalty to institutions, that obeying the Holy Spirit's voice is more important than maintaining appearances, and that protecting our spiritual health is worth a sacrifice even when it costs us something.

Often, church culture values institutional loyalty above everything else, equating leaving a church with spiritual failure and pressuring people to stay in harmful situations for the sake of "unity." These stories encourage us to trust our judgment, honor the Holy Spirit's guidance even when others don't understand, and prioritize our relationship with God over our connection to any particular community.

Perhaps the most hopeful message in these stories is that healing from church hurt is possible, even though it's rarely quick. We see this in the woman who faced deep pain and withdrew from church community altogether, worshipping at home for years because it felt "safe and fulfilling, although lonely." Her healing didn't happen overnight; it involved a pandemic that made online worship normal, a slow reconnecting with community, a move to a new state, and, finally, an invitation from her son to visit his church. When she finally found her new church home, she could declare with confidence, "I am at HOME! To God be the glory!" Still, that homecoming was the result of a long journey through isolation, searching, and gradual restoration.

Through these stories, we are taught that healing from church hurt isn't about returning to naivety or pretending the hurt never happened. Instead, it involves integrating painful experiences into our larger story, allowing them to strengthen rather than weaken our faith. It requires trusting that God can bring beauty from ashes and restoration from ruin. Healing takes time and may include seasons of withdrawal, periods of searching, moments of anger and grief, and the slow process of learning to trust again—but it is possible, and it's worth the effort.

As we close this book, the question is no longer "What happened to them?" but "What is happening to you?" What pews have you occupied on your spiritual journey? What perspectives have shaped your worship experiences? What seeds were planted in your childhood that are only now beginning to sprout? What calls have you resisted? What hurts are you carrying? What shift is the Holy Spirit inviting you to make?

Your story matters. The pew where you first felt God's presence, the moment when warmth flooded your chest, the altar where you surrendered your life to Christ, and the season of searching are all part of your unique testimony of God's faithfulness. You may be in a season of spiritual awakening, experiencing the Holy Spirit in new and powerful ways, discovering that worship isn't about where you sit but about how open your heart is to God's presence. If so, embrace it fully.

Allow yourself to be transformed. Do not mock what you do not yet understand, for you may soon find yourself dancing in the very pews where you once sat skeptically.

You might be in a season of faithful endurance, serving year after year through leadership changes, shifts in worship style, and the inevitable disappointments of being part of an imperfect community. If so, remember that your faithfulness matters. Your perseverance does not go unnoticed by God. Your example is influencing the next generation, even when you can't see the fruits of your labor.

You might be in a season of answering God's call, hearing your name spoken with increasing authority, feeling the urge to move forward even when your feet seem to resist, and fear keeps you frozen in place. If so, take courage. Rise from your seat and put one foot in front of the other. Keep your eyes fixed straight ahead, not on the churning waters of doubt. Trust the voice that calls your name and remember that what awaits you at the front of the church—transformation, a new life, and a fresh start—is worth the awkward, stumbling walk down the aisle.

You may be in a season of searching, visiting churches, and watching online services, trying to find a place that feels like home, wondering if such a place even exists. If so, don't give up. Keep seeking. Trust that the God who plants seeds in childhood will bring them to full harvest in His perfect time. Your spiritual home is out there, and when you find it, you will know that you know... that you know.

No matter what season you're in, one thing remains constant in every story in this book and every chapter of your life: God's faithfulness. He was faithful to the child crawling under the pews, to the teenager who felt a warmth in her chest but didn't understand its meaning, and to the woman who served for nine years before being cast out. God stayed faithful through church hurt, seasons of loneliness, and over 80 years of service.

And God will be faithful to you. Even when you don't understand what is happening, He will be faithful. Even when the community disappoints you, He will be faithful. Even when you stray from the path, He will be faithful. Even when you are healing, He will be faithful. Even when you are wounded, He will be faithful.

This is the core message of *Pews & Perspectives*: that our faith does not rest on the reliability of church institutions, the perfection of spiritual leaders, or the consistency of the Christian community. Instead, our faith is rooted in the unchanging nature of a God who never leaves us, never forsakes us, always calls our names, and never gives up on us.

The pews may change. The perspectives may evolve. The churches may come and go. But God remains.

So, sit in your pew—whatever or wherever that may be. Develop your unique perspective that is shaped by joy and pain, triumph and trial, awakening and hurt. Tell your story with all its complexity, honesty, and hope. And trust that the God who has been faithful to every contributor in this book will be faithful to you as well.

Your journey is not over. Your story is still being written. And the best chapters may still be ahead.

To God be the glory, now and forevermore. Amen.

Inspirational Poems That Tell the Stories

The Storm Is Passing Over

Beneath the pews, she crawled as just a child,
Exploring sacred ground with curious feet,
While mother sang in the choir, faithful and mild,
And village voices kept her life complete.

Then came the night when mockery turned to praise,
When laughter died, and Holy fire fell.
She rose from the floor in wonder and in a daze—
The Spirit's touch no human tongue could tell.

Through years of hurt when leadership failed,
When restless souls sought churches near and far,
Though loneliness and disappointment prevailed,
God's faithfulness remained her guiding star.

From Jersey pews to Texas megachurch halls,
Through online streams when pandemic doors were closed,
She answered still when Jesus gently called,
And found at last the home her heart had chosen.

Now generations worship side by side,
Her son, his wife, and their children are learning, too.
The pew baby has come full circle wide,
And God has proven His every promise true.

Eighty Years of Standing

For 80 years, she's walked this narrow road,
Through Sunday schools and choirs that raised her voice.
She's carried faith like a precious, heavy load,
And made obedience her daily choice.

They turned her from the choir box and made her weep,
Dismissed her when she spoke of stolen gold.
Yet still she rose, her covenant to keep,
Her Shepherd's love, more valuable than gold.

She buried her father with that railroad song,
Endured the pastor's rambling, painful words,
But held to Jesus when the night was long,
And found her comfort in the Shepherd's herds.

From A.M.E. traditions, firm and true
To City of Refuge's online embrace,
She's sat in every kind of church-house pew,
And seen the glory shining on God's face.

Now a great-grandmother, author, and servant still,
She writes her poems of Jesus, a Friend so dear.
Her life declares, "I've climbed that mountain hill,
And kept my hand upon the throttle here."

The Voice That Called My Name

For months, the Spirit pulled with gentle force,
A quiet voice that whispered, "Come to Me."
He sat there frozen, fighting his own course,
Super-glued to pews, afraid to be set free.

Then came that Sunday morning, clear and bright,
When "Terrace, come!" rang louder than before.
He popped up like a Jack-in-the-box in the light,
And stumbled down that red-carpeted floor.

Like Peter walking on the churning sea,
He kept his eyes fixed straight ahead, not down.
Each cement-shoed step toward destiny,
Until he reached the front and claimed his crown.

The water closed above his bended head,
And he arose a new creation, washed and clean.
The old life gone, the past forever dead,
The greatest transformation the church had ever seen.

Since 1994, that February day,
His name is written in the Book of Life.
Though sometimes still he stumbles on the way,
God's grace sustains him through each earthly strife.

Peppermints and Broken Pews

She swung her feet and sucked on peppermints,
While Madea ushered and the people shouted loud.
A little girl who didn't catch the hints,
That seeds were planted deep beneath that crowd.

The warmth came first at Windsor Village's door,
A chest that heated up with joy unknown.
She drove herself to Morning Star for more,
And watched the faith become her very own.

Nine years she served with loyalty and love,
As youth director, greeter, minister ordained.
She thought her leaders' hearts matched Heaven above,
But mean-girl spirits left her soul blood-stained.

The drama came, the rumors, false attacks,
The "conflict of interest" texts that cut so deep.
No meeting held, no leaders watching backs,
Just wounded servants left alone to weep.

But God said, "Shift!"—and though it broke her heart,
She chose obedience over comfort's call.
For healing comes when we let Jesus start,
To bind the wounds and catch us when we fall.

Inches from Eternity

A bullet flew past where her head had been,
Through flesh and screen and plaster wall it tore.
While children slept, unaware of the sin,
That nearly left them motherless and poor.

The blood she cleaned while officers took notes,
Her best friend cuffed for a crime he didn't do.
The gun's true owner fled without remorse,
Leaving chaos in his view.

"What if?" became the question haunting her nights.
"What if that bullet found me where I stood?
What if my babies woke to tragic sights?"
But God's protection proved His hand was good.

The trauma lingered long after the scene,
But whispers came: "Change the company you keep."
She cut the ties to all that came between,
Her family's safety and her faith so deep.

Now, with husband by her side and five children grown,
She testifies that God is right on time.
Through trials faced, His faithfulness was shown;
Her faith survived the test, refined and sublime.

From Ritual to Real

She sat on the back pews as a "Church Baby" blessed,
With grandmother ushering, mother in prayer,
She learned all the motions, knew how to be dressed,
But something was missing; God wasn't quite there.

For 40 long years, she went through the routine,
Sang hymns in the choir, bowed head at the right times,
She lived on faith borrowed, not hers, but between,
Two marriages failed, and unanswered prayer chimes.

She wandered through Buddhism and New Age's embrace,
Tried filling the void with philosophies new,
But emptiness lingered—she couldn't replace,
The God she knew about with the God she once knew.

Broken and desperate, alone in her room,
She cried out for real: "God, I need You tonight!
Not services, songs, or traditions that loom;
I need You to save me, to make this life right."

He whispered, "Come home," and she felt His true peace.
No longer performing or chasing the show,
She talks to Him daily, her burdens release.
Now, real religion has blossomed and continues to grow.

Meet the Authors

Compiler & Contributor

Angela R. Edwards

Foreword Writer

Pastor Abie Kulynych

Contributor

Marlowe R. Scott

Contributor

Terrace V. White

Contributor

Min. Tosha R. Dearbone

Contributor

Reyna Harris-Goynes

Contributor

Simone "Iman" Holyfield

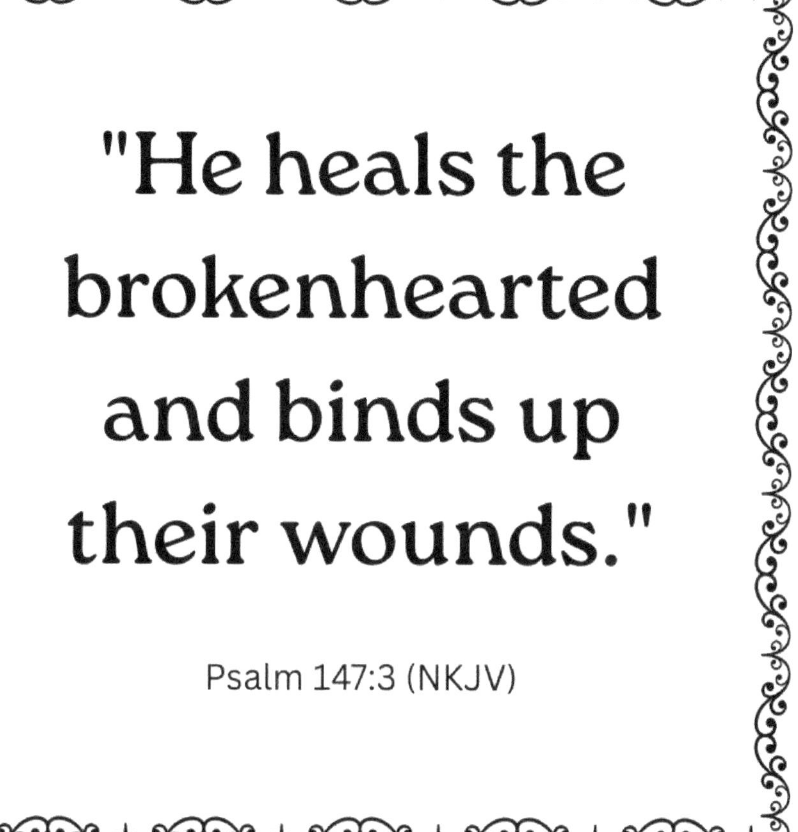
"He heals the brokenhearted and binds up their wounds."
Psalm 147:3 (NKJV)

www.ingramcontent.com/pod-product-compliance
Lightning Source LLC
LaVergne TN
LVHW010102110826
845155LV00028B/450
* 9 7 8 1 9 4 8 8 5 3 9 1 0 *